JAMES MADISON AND FREEDOM OF SPEECH

Major Debates in the Early Republic

Juhani Rudanko

University Press of America,® Inc.
Dallas · Lanham · Boulder · New York · Oxford

Copyright © 2004 by
University Press of America,® Inc.
4501 Forbes Boulevard
Suite 200
Lanham, Maryland 20706
UPA Acquisitions Department (301) 459-3366

PO Box 317
Oxford
OX2 9RU, UK

Library of Congress Control Number: 2004101005
ISBN 0-7618-2855-9 (paperback : alk. ppr.)

♾™ The paper used in this publication meets the minimum
requirements of American National Standard for Information
Sciences—Permanence of Paper for Printed Library Materials,
ANSI Z39.48—1984

Contents

Preface

Freedom of information is probably the most distinctive feature of American political culture today. It is widely recognized in the United States that the proper functioning of representative democracy requires that citizens have access to information, including information about the shortcomings of those in power, and, as a consequence, the political system is characterized by a remarkable degree of openness and accountability. By contrast, European political systems tend to be more opaque. Instead of openness and accountability, there are official secrets acts and other barriers designed to restrict the free flow of information.

The American culture of openness and accountability is ultimately enshrined in the First Amendment, with its unique language restricting the power of the national Legislature. The present book sheds light on the question of how this icon of free speech came to be enacted and how freedom of speech survived the challenge of the Sedition Act of 1798.

James Madison is of course well known as the father of the Bill of Rights. However, his crucial role in the procedural debates in the summer of 1789 has not been sufficiently appreciated in the literature. Rudanko (2003) sought to remedy this lack of recognition but that book also had a focus on fallacy theory, and there was a need for a follow-up volume concentrating on the overall structure of argumentation in the key Bill of Rights and Sedition Act debates in the important period from 1789 to 1801. The present book aims to fill this gap. It also seeks to ensure that the stature and significance of James Madison as probably the greatest political philosopher ever should come to appreciated more widely.

It gives me great pleasure here to acknowledge the hospitality that I have enjoyed in a number of departments — English, Communication, History, Philosophy, Linguistics — at the University of Arizona in recent years. Scott Jacobs, of the Department of Communication of the University of Arizona, kindly read chapter 3 of the present book. At the University of Tampere in Finland, Lea Luodes helped me conscientiously with the checking of source materials and the compiling of the index, and Ian Gurney kindly commented on several chapters of this book.

None of the persons identified in the previous paragraph is in any way responsible for the contents of this book. That responsibility rests entirely with me, being the sole author of the book.

Tampere, Finland
Juhani Rudanko

Chapter 1

Introduction

Examining freedom of speech and its role in contemporary America in a recent book, Rodney Smolla identifies a number of different functions that it fulfils. One of them is linked to the theory of the "marketplace of ideas": "humankind's search for truth is best advanced by a free trade of ideas" (Smolla 1992, 6)). Another important function that freedom of speech serves in civilized countries today is to contribute to a sense of human dignity, for "freedom to speak without restraint provides the speaker with an inner satisfaction and realization of self-identity essential to individual fulfillment" (Smolla (1992, 9), note omitted).

Further, freedom of speech is essential to the functioning of democratic and representative self-government. Smolla describes one aspect of this facet of freedom of speech as follows:

> It is through nonviolent speech that the people may ferret out corruption and discourage tyrannical excesses, keeping government within the metes and bounds of the charter through which the people first brought it into existence. (Smolla (1992, 13))

In view of the considerations briefly sketched on the basis of Smolla's recent treatment, it is easy to see why freedom of speech is generally recognized to be a most fundamental right of individuals in civilized countries today. It should also be noted that freedom of speech is a peculiarly American contribution to modern civilization, and it is in the United States that individuals continue to enjoy the highest degree of freedom of speech today.

The unique openness that is a characteristic of American political culture ultimately traces its origins to the American Bill of Rights, proposed by James Madison to the first House of Representatives in the summer of 1789. There were two provisions relating to freedom of speech that Madison proposed on June 8, 1789. Here is one of them:

> The people shall not be deprived or abridged of their right to speak, to write, or to publish their sentiments; and the freedom of the press, as one of the great bulwarks of liberty, shall be inviolable. (Gales (1834, 434))

And here is the other:

> No State shall violate the equal rights of conscience, or the freedom of the press, or
> the trial by jury in criminal cases. (Gales (1834, 435))

The second of these amendments, esteemed by Madison as the most valuable of all the amendments (Gales (1834, 755)),[1] was passed by the House of Representatives but rejected by the Senate. The first, for its part, did survive and was enshrined in the memorable language of the First Amendment, ratified in 1791:

> Congress shall make no law respecting an establishment of religion, or prohibit the
> free exercise thereof; or abridging the freedom of speech, or of the press; or of the
> right of the people peaceably to assemble, and to petition the Government for a
> redress of grievance. (Article I of the Federal Bill of Rights, as promulgated on
> December 15, 1791, see Rutland (1983, 243))

A number of other countries have legal or constitutional provisions that are often claimed to be aimed at safeguarding freedom of speech today, and there does undoubtedly exist some degree of freedom of speech in a number of countries in the world today. However, the unique feature of the American Bill of Rights is that it places a restriction on the power of the legislative branch of Government, whereas provisions ostensibly aimed at safeguarding freedom of speech in other countries, while often rich in rhetoric, do not involve any analogous restriction on the power of the Legislature. This means that in such countries the Legislature, having no limit on its power, is easily able to "define" — that is, to restrict — freedom of speech in ways that it sees fit.

Because of its unique character, the Bill of Rights serves to guarantee a unique degree of freedom of speech in the United States.[2] It also has an impact outside the United States, as has been remarked on by perceptive commentators. For instance, here is Bernard Levin writing in *The Times* of London in August 1991:

> ... that splendid organization, the Campaign for Freedom of Information, has just
> revealed disturbing facts about the tests for pollution from pharmaceutical plants in
> Britain—a matter, surely, that potentially concerns us all. Not so; the Campaign's
> revelation is prohibited on pain of two year's imprisonment. But the Campaign's
> leaders will not go to chokey; they got the information from the United States
> Freedom of Information Act, not from Britain. Americans, you see, are trusted by
> their government; we are not fit to know whether we are going to be poisoned.
>
> The Campaign has revealed a wide range of such British information garnered
> from America; this month's broadsheet is devoted to the subject and readers will
> begin to think they are hallucinating, so ridiculous and so scandalous are the things
> Americans can tell us that we cannot be told by our own governors. (Levin (1991,

14))

The purpose of this book is to examine a formative stage in the process that led to the American concept of freedom of speech. The book sheds new light on James Madison's unique role in shaping that concept in the period from 1789 till 1801 by examining patterns of argumentation in key debates of the period and Madison's role in the debates.

Turning to the individual chapters, chapter 2 provides background for later chapters, with an emphasis on developments prior to 1789. The chapter introduces major doctrines that had restricted freedom of speech in Great Britain, including the doctrine of seditious libel. The chapter also introduces, in an eclectic fashion, some of James Madison's early ideas on the question of how to secure the liberty of individuals, and other issues bearing on freedom of speech, including an exchange during James Madison's election campaign for a seat in the first House of Representatives, when he ran against another future President, James Monroe.

The debates and statements examined in the later chapters have been selected because they are especially important to the development of the American concept of freedom of speech.

Chapter 3 offers a detailed analysis of the debate of June 8, 1789. On that date James Madison presented his proposals for a Bill of Rights, and made his major substantive speech in support of the project of amendments. Federalists had an overwhelming majority in the first House of Representatives over Antifederalists, and Madison, one of the authors of the Federalist Papers, was of course a leading Federalist at this time.

Madison's proposals received a hostile reaction from his fellow Representatives in the first House of Representatives. It is not true, as has sometimes been alleged, that no one else supported his proposals in the debate of June 8, 1789. However, the response was overwhelmingly hostile or at least skeptical, both from Federalists and Antifederalists, and Madison had to exercise all his rhetorical skills to keep the project of amendments from being killed on that day.

The long debate of June 8, 1789 did not concern the substance of the amendments. Instead it was a debate about whether to debate or not, being focused on the procedural issue of whether or not to debate Madison's propositions at all in a timely fashion. In the course of the discussion a proposal was made by the Federalist Representative James Jackson to postpone any consideration of the subject till the following March. It is argued that the true purpose of Jackson's proposal was to kill Madison's project. Fallacy theory is introduced in this context to analyze some of the arguments put forward in the debate.

Madison's project survived the ordeal of June 8, 1789, but two other procedural debates — again debates about whether or not to debate the issue of amendments — were still to follow. These took place on July 21 and August 13, 1789. In both of them the fate of the project hung precariously in the balance. Chapters 4 and 5 examine the nature of argumentation, both for and against considering Madison's project, in these further procedural debates.

Ultimately, James Madison was successful and the first House of Representatives did end the sequence of procedural debates and decided to consider the substance of the Bill of Rights, but it was a close call. The prolonged procedural wrangling is in itself indicative of the reluctance with which some members of the House of Representatives, especially some Federalists, viewed Madison's project in the summer of 1789. Taking account of the fact that once the procedural hurdle had been passed, the House of Representatives acted with impressive speed, it is possible to say that the procedural debates, considered here in chapters 3 to 5, were among the most critical stages in the history of the Bill of Rights.

In this part of the book the focus is on the nature of Federalist objections and on the question of how Madison was able to persuade the House of Representatives to proceed with the consideration of the Bill of Rights.

The adoption of the amendments in the House of Representatives created an incentive for the Senate to act. No doubt there were hurdles in the way of the project in the Senate, but unfortunately the Senate met in secret at that time and records of Senate debates cannot be studied in the same way as House debates can be.

Chapter 6 moves beyond the enactment of the Bill of Rights to a debate in 1794 that is also highly significant from the point of view of freedom of speech. In the aftermath of disturbances in the four Western counties of Pennsylvania, the so-called Whiskey Rebellion, President Washington had made a remark on Democratic Societies and the House of Representatives got embroiled in a long debate about whether to censure such societies in its response to the President. The Federalist Party was still dominant at this time, but the opposition was now made up of Jeffersonian Republicans, with James Madison a leading Republican. The chapter examines arguments used by the two sides in these debates.

Chapter 7 takes up the enactment of the Sedition Act of 1798. Two major debates took place in the House of Representatives in the first half of July 1798, before the Act was approved. Federalists were the driving force behind the Act, while Republicans were opposed to it. Arguments put forward by the two sides in the debates are examined in the chapter.

Chapters 8 and 9 examine two later contributions to the debates surrounding the Sedition Act and the concept of freedom of speech at that time. Chapter 8 deals with a statement of the Federalist position from February 1799, and chapter 9 looks at the exposition of Madison's views in the Report of 1800. It is seen that both statements were highly significant from the point of view of the concept of freedom of speech.

Chapter 10 examines an event that has generally been overlooked in work on early American history and even in work on the Sedition Act. This was a Federalist attempt in January 1801 to make the Sedition Act permanent. When it was enacted in 1798, the Sedition Act had a time limit on it, but when the time approached for it to lapse, Federalists made it clear that they wanted to make it permanent. The chapter examines the nature of Federalist argumentation in the debates for the perpetuation of the Act, extending over several days. It should be noted that the debates took place before the election of Thomas Jefferson, at a time when the future of freedom of speech again hung in the balance in the new Republic. Even though research on freedom of speech has tended to overlook these debates, the major figures of the Federalist Party took an active part in them, and there is no doubt that Federalists were serious in their attempt to enact a permanent Sedition Act.

Chapter 11 draws together two themes of this volume, commenting on what the Congressional debates examined can tell us about original intent and also commenting on the constitutive power of the Bill of Rights.

A comment may be appended here on the relation of the present book to earlier work by the present author. Sometimes debates are examined that were also examined in earlier work, especially in Rudanko (2003). However, in earlier publications the focus was on specific linguistic or rhetorical features, especially the nature and use of fallacies in certain debates. Such rhetorical features are likewise noted in the present book where they are salient. (The concept of a fallacy is discussed in chapter 3.) However, in the present volume the focus is on the overall nature of argumentation in the debates, whether or not the arguments in question involved distinctive linguistic or rhetorical features or not.

In all the debates examined in this book there were always two identifiable parties involved opposing each other's point of view, and the Reports of February 1799 and 1800 also represent statements from opposing sides in the dispute over the Sedition Act and over the meaning of the concept of freedom of speech. Examining the overall nature of argumentation employed in the key debates from 1789 till 1801 thus means examining themes — assumptions made and patterns of reasoning used — in the arguments put forward by the opposing sides in the disputes in question. There is some overlap between this book and earlier publications, but such overlap can be kept within reasonable bounds because of the distinctive focus of the present book.

It is also worth noting, to emphasize the distinctiveness of the present book, that there are debates and contributions covered here that were not covered in the present author's earlier work at all. This holds for instance for the debates of November 1794 and the Federalist statement of February 1799. The present book should be seen as complementing earlier work, but it is offered as an independent study.

Notes to Chapter 1

1. It seems possible to relate Madison's lost amendment to an important sentiment that he, assisted by Alexander Hamilton, had expressed in The Federalist No. 20, at the end of a long survey of badly functioning confederacies:

> The important truth ... is, that a sovereignty over sovereigns, a government over governments, a legislation for communities, as contradistinguished from individuals; as it is a solecism in theory; so in practice, it is subversive of the order and ends of civil polity, by substituting *violence* in place of *law,* or the destructive *coertion* of the *sword,* in place of the mild and salutary *coertion* of the *magistracy.* (Cooke, ed. (1961, 128 f.), the emphasis in the original)

Madison was arguing "that confederation in which the subunits are the sovereign entities, and the central government lacks the power to act directly on individuals, is repeatedly a failure" (Miller (1992, 19 f.)). The lost amendment derived from his insight that there is a need for a direct connection between the central government and individuals.

2. That is, the American Bill of Rights serves to guarantee a unique degree of freedom of speech in the United States today. The Bill of Rights did not immediately assume the role that it has today. One reason was no doubt the rejection of the amendment that was directed against encroachment by the States. William Lee Miller provides this commentary:

> Had Madison's "Lost Amendment" been ratified, the history of American constitutional law—and therefore of human rights in the United States—would certainly have been different. ... The protection of liberties against the states (and all subordinate units) by the federal bill of rights had to wait until after the Civil War. In the aftermath of the victory over the secessionists, the Fourteenth Amendment was added to the Constitution, providing in its most important provision that "no *state* shall deprive any citizen of life, liberty, or property, without due process of the laws." This passage from the Fourteenth Amendment of 1868 was to be the most important addition to the Constitution after these amendments of 1789. It would pick up the term *due process of law* that Madison had already used in what was to become the Fifth Amendment, linked to the three-term series from John Locke: ["]No person shall ... be deprived of life, liberty, or property; without due process of law." That phrase of Madison's, like the "necessary and proper" clause in the body of the Constitution, was one of those small openings through which passed a vast development of governing, of thought, and of life—in this case, of protections of liberty. ...
>
> The application of the federal Bill of Rights to the states, in practical fact, would not follow directly upon the ratification of the Fourteenth Amendment in the late nineteenth century, but would wait until the middle of the twentieth century, when the Supreme Court would interpret the "liberty" one is not to be deprived of

without "due process of law" as "incorporating" some, or all—the argument continues—of the liberties protected by the first eight amendments of the federal Bill of Rights. (Miller (1992, 254 f.), the emphases in the original)

Chapter 2
The Historical Background

The British Background

Looking back on British and Western European history, it is remarkable how little freedom of speech individual human beings enjoyed in the centuries following the invention of printing. Here is a summary of this aspect of political and legal history by Justice Story:

> The art of printing soon after its introduction ... was looked upon, as well in England as in other countries, as merely a matter of state, and subject to the coercion of the crown. It was, therefore, regulated in England by the King's proclamations, prohibitions, charters of privilege, and licenses, and finally by the decrees of the Court of the Star-Chamber, which limited the number of printers and of presses which each should employ, and prohibited new publications, unless previously approved by proper licensers. On the demolition of this odious jurisdiction, in 1641, the Long Parliament of Charles the First, after their rupture with that prince, assumed the same powers which the Star-Chamber exercised with respect to licensing books; and during the Commonwealth (such is human frailty and the love of power even in republics!) they issued their ordinances for that purpose, founded principally upon a Star-Chamber decree in 1637. After the restoration of Charles the Second, a statute on the same subject was passed, copied, with some few alterations, from the parliamentary ordinances. (quoted from Nowak and Rotunda (1991, 936))

The licensing law that Justice Story mentions expired in the wake of the Glorious Revolution in 1694. However, it is also important to take note of the law of seditious libel as a law restricting freedom of speech in England:

> The publication of statements critical of the sovereign or his agents was considered seditious libel. The theory of the action, as developed in the Court of the Star Chamber and utilized in subsequent common law courts, was that the King, as the originator of justice, was above popular criticism. Publication of opinions that were censorious of the government constituted, therefore, a criminal assault. Truth was not a defense, for "the greater the truth, the greater the libel" against the government. [note omitted] (Nowak and Rotunda (1991, 935))

In spite of severe limitations on freedom of speech, there have been individuals who have felt a desire for free public debate and a desire for access to information and to knowledge. A breakthrough of some significance occurred with the English Bill of Rights of 1689. This is a wordy document, but it contains the following key provisions:

> And thereupon the said lords spiritual and temporal and commons, pursuant to their respective letters and elections being now assembled in a full and free representative of this nation, ... do in the first place (as their ancestors in like case have usually done) for the vindicating and asserting their ancient rights and liberties, declare that the pretended power of suspending of laws or the execution of laws by regal authority without consent of parliament is illegal; ... that election of members of parliament ought to be free; that the freedom of speech and debates or proceedings in parliament ought not to be impeached or questioned in any court or place out of parliament; ... (Stephenson and Marcham (1972, 601))

The English Bill of Rights thus granted a large measure of freedom of speech to members of the British Parliament in their speeches in Parliament. Its provisions did not grant any measure of freedom of speech to individuals who were not members of Parliament.

At the same time, it would be a mistake to suppose that there was complete control of publications in eighteenth-century England. Writings advocating a measure of freedom of speech were not totally suppressed, or at least they were not suppressed with the harshness and ruthless brutality that is associated with modern-day oppression, as practiced in a number of countries under communism. Among writings that were published and republished in eighteenth-century England were *Cato's Letters*. These include such lines as the following:

> Freedom of Speech is the great Bulwark of Liberty; they prosper and die together. And it is the Terror of Traytors and Oppressors, and a Barrier against them. It produces excellent Writers, and encourages Men of fine Genius. (*Cato's Letters*, February 4, 1720, in Trenchard and Gordon, eds., 1971, vol. I, 100 f.)

Two years later Cato wrote:

> If Men be suffered to preach or reason publickly and freely upon certain Subjects, as for Instance, upon Philosophy, Religion, or Government, they may reason wrongly, irreligiously, or seditiously, and sometimes will do so; and by such Means may possibly now and then pervert and mislead an ignorant and unwary Person; and if they be suffered to write their Thoughts, the Mischief may be still more diffusive; but if they be not permitted, by any or all these Ways, to communicate their Opinions or

Improvements to one another, the World must soon be over-run with Barbarism, Superstition, Injustice, Tyranny, and the most stupid Ignorance. They will know nothing of the Nature of Government beyond a servile Submission to Power; ... (*Cato's Letters,* February 27, 1722, in Trenchard and Gordon, eds., 1971, vol. II, 296 f.))

Such views were generally accompanied with praise of liberty in England in *Cato's Letters,* as in "God be thanked, we *Englishmen* have neither lost our Liberties, nor are in Danger of losing them" (*Cato's Letters,* February 4, 1720, in Trenchard and Gordon, eds., 1971, vol. I, 103), emphasis in the original). The praise tempered the force of the rhetoric supporting freedom of expression, suggesting that no change of existing practices was being advocated. For its part, the doctrine of seditious libel continued to be enforced and there continued to be prosecutions and trials of those who wrote or published criticism of the the government in eighteenth-century England (see e.g. Smith (1988, 26 f.)).

The Constitutional Convention and its Aftermath

Turning the discussion to the American context, one of the earliest major developments was the Virginia Declaration of Rights of 1776. The Declaration had this provision:

12. That freedom of the press is one of the great bulwarks of liberty, and can never be restrained but by despotick governments. (Lloyd and Lloyd 1998, 190)

It is well known that there was a serious attempt initiated by George Mason of Virginia and Elbridge Gerry of Massachusetts at the Constitutional Convention in Philadelphia in the summer of 1787 to include a Bill of Rights in the new Constitution. If the attempt had succeeded, there is little doubt that the Bill of Rights would have included a provision for freedom of speech. However, the attempt was peremptorily and decisively voted down, not receiving the vote of a single State.

The rejection of a Bill of Rights at the Constitutional Convention did not end calls for such a law, including a provision for freedom of speech. The rejection was a factor why George Mason refused to sign the new Constitution.

After the Constitutional Convention the new Constitution was submitted to the individual States for ratification. The ratification debates brought into a sharper focus the formation of two distinctive political parties in the early Republic, the Federalists and Antifederalists. Members of the former had dominated the Constitutional Convention. They were only too conscious of the weaknesses of the Confederacy and generally looked to develop the United States into a powerful country with a strong central government, according to the model of major European powers. They were in favor of ratifying the new Constitution without modifying it. For their part, Antifederalists were much less sympathetic to the establishment of a strong central government, instead wishing for the States to retain a high degree of political power. Antifederalists were cool towards the new Constitution, wishing to amend it even before it was ratified.

Regarding the nature of amendments proposed during ratification debates, it is useful to make a distinction between two broad types. A provision for safeguarding freedom of expression is an example of an amendment designed to secure the rights of individual human beings against encroachment by Federal or State authorities, and rights based amendments are one type of amendment. Such amendments have often been called procedural in the literature. There were also other types of amendments being proposed that would have strengthened the powers of State governments at the expense of the Federal level. Such amendments are often called structural in the literature.

Structural amendments were anathema to Federalists, while Antifederalists were favorable to them. As for procedural amendments, Antifederalists in general were also in favor of these, while Federalists tended to be cooler towards them, at least while the new Constitution remained to be ratified.

James Madison's Concern with Securing Liberty

James Madison's position deserves a more detailed comment at this point. He was a most prominent Federalist at this time. One reflection of his prominence was the fact that he was one of the authors of the Federalist papers. He had voted against the motion by Gerry and Mason at the Constitutional Convention for a consideration of a Bill of Rights. In the aftermath of the Convention he remained opposed to introducing amendments to the Constitution, either of the procedural or the structural type, before it was ratified. However, even at this time he combined this attitude with a keen sensitivity to the rights of individual human beings and with a concern for securing such rights. He gave expression to his concern in the Federalist Papers. Paper 10, in particular, written by Madison in late 1787, deserves to be reviewed here.

The theme of the paper is set by Madison in the opening sentence: "Among the numerous advantages promised by a well constructed Union, none deserves to be more accurately developed than its tendency to break and control the violence of faction" (Cooke, ed. (1961, 56)). A little later he defines a faction as follows:

> By a faction I understand a number of citizens, whether amounting to a majority or
> minority of the whole, who are united and actuated by some common impulse of
> passion, or of interest, adverse to the rights of other citizens, or to the permanent and

aggregate interests of the community. (Cooke, ed. (1961, 57))

Having defined faction, he proceeds to discuss the question of how to prevent the mischiefs of faction:

> There are two methods of curing the mischiefs of faction: the one, by removing its causes; the other, by controling its effects.
>
> There are again two methods of removing the causes of faction: the one, by destroying the liberty which is essential to its existence; the other, by giving to every citizen the same opinions, the same passions, and the same interests.
>
> It could never be more truly said than of the first remedy, that it was worse than the disease. Liberty is to faction, what air is to the fire, an aliment without which it instantly expires. But it could not be a less folly to abolish liberty, which is essential to political life, because it nourishes faction, than it would be to wish the annihilation of air, which is essential to animal life, because it imparts to fire its destructive agency.
>
> The second expedient is as impracticable, as the first would be unwise. As long as the reason of man continues fallible, and he is at liberty to exercise it, different opinions will be formed. As long as the connection subsists between his reason and his self-love, his opinions and his passions will have a reciprocal influence on each other; and the former will be objects to which the latter attach themselves. The diversity in the faculties of men from which the rights of property originate, is not less an insuperable obstacle to a uniformity of interests. The protection of these faculties is the first object of Government. (Cooke, ed. (1961, 58))

The comparison of liberty with the air that human beings breathe brings out the emphasis that Madison placed on the liberty of individuals.

Later in the same essay Madison makes an important point about how to safeguard the rights of individuals:

> The smaller the society, the fewer probably will be the distinct parties and interests composing it; the fewer the distinct parties and interests, the more frequently will a majority be found of the same party; and the smaller the number of individuals composing a majority, and the smaller the compass within which they are placed, the more easily will they concert and execute their plans of oppression. Extend the sphere, and you take in a greater variety of parties and interests; you make it less probable that a majority of the whole will have a common motive to invade the rights of other citizens; or if such a common motive exists, it will be more difficult for all who feel it to discover their own strength, and to act in unison with each other. Besides other impediments, it may be remarked, that where there is a consciousness of unjust or dishonorable purposes, communication is always checked by distrust, in proportion to the number whose concurrence is necessary. (Cooke, ed. (1961, 63 f.))

Here Madison makes a powerful case showing why the liberty of individuals is intrinsically more secure in a large country, rather than a small one.

The Election of the First House of Representatives

In the run-up to the elections to the first United States House of Representatives, the issue of amendments and of a Bill of Rights played a significant role. Kenneth Bowling writes:

> The procedural or civil liberty amendments drew support from those who thought that the Constitution should include a Bill of Rights like many of the state constitutions. At first most Federalists opposed such amendments. James Wilson had stated their position in December in 1788 when he argued that since the Constitution contained only delegated powers, Congress could not deprive the people of their civil liberties. But the Antifederalists and Thomas Jefferson refused to accept this argument. Even committed Federalists were divided: Charles Pinckney and Hugh Williamson had supported a Bill of Rights in the Federal Convention. To Anglo Saxons of a Revolutionary generation, the protection of civil liberties seemed only proper, and this sentiment proved the most important drawing card for the Antifederalist demand for amendments. Among the procedural proposals were protection for the freedoms of speech, assembly, petition, press, religion, and conscience, and the right to jury trial, to carry weapons, to confront witnesses at trials, to have defense counsel, and to abstention from military service for religious objectors. ...
>
> There had been little that was national about the first congressional election aside from the issue of amendments to the Constitution. This issue was central to the elections in Pennsylvania and Maryland, in several of the districts in Virginia, Massachusetts, and New York, and undoubtedly in parts of New Hampshire and South Carolina. (Bowling (1990, 125 ff.))

Regarding the question of how the two parties stood on the issue, Bowling writes:

> ... there was a clear difference between Federal and Antifederal supporters of amendments in this election: while some Federalists, when pressed, said they supported amendments, the Antifederalists promised to fight for them and constantly brought them up as an issue they knew they knew the Federalists wished to avoid. Where amendments were not the major issue, either the important candidates were all Federalists (Georgia; Charleston district, South Carolina; and Essex district, Massachusetts) or, conversely, all the candidates had to favor amendments to be

considered seriously in the campaign (Worcester district, Massachusetts). There was no contest between Federalists and Antifederalists in which amendments were not crucial. [Note omitted, JR.] (Bowling (1990, 128))

One contest where amendments played a role was the contest in the fifth district of Virginia. The contest there pitted James Madison against James Monroe. The contest turned out to be of incalculable significance, because of the role that Madison assumed in the House of Representatives. It is worth sampling two documents from this campaign between the two future Presidents. Here is the text of an appeal from the Monroe campaign:

> Gent.
>
> My solicitude for the liberty of my County constrains me to Call your attention to the Subject of Electing a Representative for this District to Congress under the General Government[.] you are sensible that the Constitution in its present form has not the hearts and affections of the people: Their fears and apprehensions are greatly alarmed and in my opinion Very justly: the Convention in June last at the Same time they Ratified it, agreed it was so far defective as to Require a Bill of Rights and a number of Amendments which you Cannot be Strangers to: ... I hope you will Consider the Necessity of uniting in favor of a Gent. who has been uniformly in favour of Amendments I mean James Monroe Esq. a man who possesses great abilities integrity and a most amiable Character who has been many years a member of Congress of the House of Delegats and of the Privy Council and whome I have Prevaled on to offer in our District, Considering him as being able to Render his Country great Servises on this important occasion. it is now Submitted to your Consideration whether you wish for amendments or not, and if you do who is the most likely to obtain them, the man who has been uniformly in favor of them, or one who has been uniformly against them. [...] (DenBoer et al. (1984, 329 f.))

The election appeal is revealing: James Madison is not referred to by name, but there is no doubt that when speaking of "the one who has been uniformly against them," that is, against amendments, the author of the appeal wishes to refer to James Madison. By contrast, James Monroe is extolled as the one "most likely to obtain them."

James Madison had voted against the consideration of a Bill of Rights at the Constitutional Convention in the summer of 1787. There had been some signs of flexibility in his position since then. For instance, such signs surfaced in the summer of 1788 when the new Constitution faced opposition when being debated in Virginia prior to being approved. However, the election appeal testifies to a continuing perception of James Madison as an opponent of amendments at the time of the appeal, dated "c. January 1789" by DenBoer et al. (1984).

At about this time Madison made a pledge that turned out to be a world historical importance. Writing to a potential supporter, he said in part:

> Being informed that reports prevail not only that I am opposed to any amendments whatever to the new federal Constitution, but that I have ceased to be a friend to the rights of Conscience; and inferring from a conversation with my brother William, that you are disposed to contradict such reports as far as your knowledge of my sentiments may justify, I am led to trouble you with this communication of them. ...
>
> I freely own that I have never seen in the Constitution as it now stands those serious dangers which have alarmed many respectable Citizens. Accordingly whilst it remained unratified, and it was necessary to unite the States in some one plan, I opposed all previous alterations as calculated to throw the States into dangerous contentions, and to furnish the Secret enemies of the Union with an opportunity of promoting its dissolution. Circumstances are now changed: The Constitution is established on the ratifications of eleven States and a very great majority of the people of America, and amendments, if pursued with a proper moderation and in a proper mode, will be not only safe, but may serve the double purpose of satisfying the minds of well meaning opponents, and of providing additional guards in favour of liberty. Under this change of circumstances, it is my sincere opinion that the Constitution ought to be revised, and that the first Congress meeting under it, ought to prepare and recommend to the States for ratification, the most satisfactory provisions for all essential rights, particularly the rights of Conscience in the fullest latitude, the freedom of the press, trials by jury, security against general warrants &c. (DenBoer et al. (1984, 330 f.))

The question of why Madison made his promise is a fascinating one, but one that can probably never be solved with absolute certainty. The election campaign may well have served to focus his mind on the issue of amendments, and no doubt his correspondence with his friend Thomas Jefferson also played a role. It is also reasonable to give credence to the reason that he gave, that the ratification of the Constitution had created a situation where it was possible to approve a Bill of Rights, because of his generally upright character. Another consideration lending credibility to Madison's stated reason is his remarkable sensitivity to the rights of individual human beings, as shown in Federalist Paper Number 10, reviewed above.

James Madison thus made a promise during the election campaign to support amendments of the procedural type and a Bill of Rights to safeguard them. However, not all Federalists by any means followed suit. Bowling writes:

> ... there were still some Federalists such as Robert Morris, Roger Sherman, and Ralph Izard, who did not sanction amendments in any form. Benjamin Rush supported John Adams for the vice-presidency not only because he hoped Adams would support

Philadelphia as the permanent residence of Congress, but also because he counted on Adams to protect the nation from amendments and a second convention. [Note omitted, JR] (Bowling (1990, 129))

Federalists scored a triumphant victory in the elections to the first United States House of Representatives, with Madison being among the winning candidates. The victory meant that the issue of amendments and of a Bill of Rights hung finely in the balance when the first Congress met in the spring of 1789. The stage was set for one of the most important Congressional debates ever.

Chapter 3

James Madison and the Debate of June 8, 1789

On Monday, June 8, 1789 James Madison moved that the House of Representatives should begin to consider amendments. Here is the record of this first speech:

> Mr. Madison rose, and reminded the House that this was the day that he had heretofore named for bringing forward amendments to the Constitution, as contemplated in the fifth article of the Constitution. He then addressed the Speaker as follows: This day, Mr. Speaker, is the day assigned for taking into consideration the subject of amendments to the Constitution. As I considered myself bound in honor and in duty to do what I have done on this subject, I shall proceed to bring the amendments before you as soon as possible and advocate them until they shall be finally adopted or rejected by a Constitutional majority of this House. With a view of drawing your attention to this important object, I shall move that this House do now resolve itself into a Committee of the Whole on the State of the Union; by which an opportunity will be given, to bring forward some propositions, which I have strong hopes will meet with the unanimous approbation of this House, after the fullest discussion and most serious regard. I therefore move you that the House now go into a committee on this business. (Gales (1834, 424))

In this initial speech Madison said that he considered himself "bound in honor and in duty" to acting in the matter of amendments, and went on to propose that amendments should be considered in a timely fashion and that this should be done by way of the House of Representatives acting as a Committee of the Whole. The mode of the House of Representatives acting as a Committee of the Whole on the State of the Union was procedural. Madison's desire to consider amendments in a timely fashion was also ostensibly procedural, but given the vagaries of shifting circumstances and the limited duration of Congressional sessions, it also had a substantive element to it.

Both parts of what Madison wanted to do ran into immediate and fierce opposition. The next speaker was William Smith, Federalist of South Carolina. (The attribution is made on the basis of *The Gazette of the United States,* June 10,

1789.) He opposed Madison's motion for going into a Committee of the Whole. Instead, he noted that there were two ways of introducing the business, by way of a select committee or by Madison getting his propositions printed, to be "taken up for discussion at a future day" (Gales (1834, 425)). However, he argued that "it must appear extremely impolitic to go into the consideration of amending the Government, before it is organized, before it has begun to operate" (Gales (1834, 425)). He argued further that "if we go into the discussion of this subject, it will take us three weeks or a month; and during all this time, every other business must be suspended" (Gales (1834, 425)).

James Jackson's Rhetorical Questions

The next speaker was Mr. Jackson, who made a long speech that deserves close scrutiny. The full text of the speech is given in the appendix to the chapter. An obvious feature of the speech is the presence in it, in abundance, of rhetorical questions. Here are one or two from early in the speech:

> What experience have we had of the good or bad qualities of this Constitution? Can any gentleman affirm to me one proposition that is a certain and absolute amendment? I deny that he can. Our Constitution, sir, is like a vessel just launched, and lying at the wharf; she is untried, you can hardly discover any one of her properties. It is not known how she will answer her helm, or lay her course; whether she will bear with safety the precious freight to be deposited in her hold. But, in this state, will the prudent merchant attempt alterations? Will he employ workmen to tear off the planking and take asunder the frame? He certainly will not. (Gales (1834, 425))

Rhetorical questions have the form of questions and are therefore directed at an audience, at least ostensibly. Thus at one level they enhance audience involvement in a speech even though the format of the interaction is a speech and the speaker is well aware that he has the floor.

To get a better purchase on the nature and the use of a rhetorical question, it is useful to start from a definition. In the literature a standard definition of a rhetorical question is to say that a rhetorical question is one where "the answer is a foregone conclusion" (Quirk (1985, 1478)). It is in fact possible to say that the speaker intends the expected answer to be obvious or "a foregone conclusion."

Given such speaker intentions, it is helpful to view rhetorical questions as challenges, when used in a discourse intended to be persuasive:

> ... rhetorical questions are challenges made by the speaker to the hearer. The hearer challenges the hearer to accept (concur with) or to reject (counter) the expected answer to the rhetorical question. It is important to add that the options are not on a

par. There is a strong expectation for the hearer to concur with rather than to reject the expected answer, ... (Rudanko (1995, 398))

The expectation for the hearer to agree rather than to disagree is partly based on a general tendency to be co-operative in interactive discourse. As Keith Allan puts it:

Since it is co-operative to go along with one's interlocutor, H [the hearer, JR] will tend to maintain S's [the speaker's, JR] positive face by not disputing a rhetorical question ..., even if he is given the chance.[1] (Allan (1986, 223))

While there may be a tendency to agree rather than to disagree generally operative in interactive discourse, the strength of the tendency as a constraint on the behavior of interlocutors is hardly constant and is a function of a number of factors, including the genre of discourse and the mutual relations of participants in a particular discourse. The tendency may be an important factor favoring agreement in a conversation among friends who are sensitive to the needs of each other. However, in argumentative political rhetoric between adherents of two standpoints the role of the tendency, it seems safe to assume, is not particularly strong.

There is a second factor that probably plays a more significant role in a genre such as political discourse that tends to be adversarial. This is more language specific:

The speaker typically phrases his or her rhetorical question in such a way that the expected answer is the only reasonable and logical one, given the terms of the question. (Rudanko (1995, 398))

In the sample above, James Jackson's choice of the adjectives *certain* and *absolute* is significant from this point of view:

Given the difficulty of phrasing amendments, Jackson must have been confident that no 'absolute' amendment could have been forthcoming and that a negative answer was the only reasonable one. (Rudanko (1995, 398))

The discussion of rhetorical questions so far has emphasized the point that the speaker wants the hearer to accept the expected answer as obvious and as the only reasonable answer possible, and that this effect may come about on account of a general tendency to agree rather than to disagree with the speaker or on account of the rather leading nature of the question. The two features, with the same aim, are mutually reinforcing and complementary to each other.

However, in discourse that is intended to be persuasive, getting the audience to accept the propositional content of the expected answer may not be the full point or purpose of a rhetorical question. To assess this issue, we may ask whether Jackson would have rested satisfied if his audience had agreed for instance with the intended answers of his first two rhetorical questions, namely with the proposition 'we have had no experience of the good or bad qualities of this Constitution' as the answer to the question "What experience have we had of the good or bad qualities of this Constitution?" and with 'no' as the answer to the second rhetorical question "Can any gentleman affirm to me one proposition that is a certain and absolute amendment?"

To get a better overall view of the nature and function of a rhetorical question in argumentative discourse, it is worth quoting Ilie's work at this point:

> ... the addresser of a rhetorical question does not only know its answer, but is also committed to it and intends thereby to reinforce, qualify or cancel the addressee's beliefs, assumptions, opinions, etc.; its ultimate goal is to motivate the addressee, viz. to induce in the addressee a similar commitment and thus the disposition and willingness to act accordingly ... (Ilie, (1994, 45))

The point that the goal of a rhetorical question is to affect the beliefs of the addressee and to induce a "willingness to act accordingly," is valuable. Applied to the first rhetorical question in Jackson's speech, it is possible to make the following comment:

> It seems clear that all members of the House of Representatives agreed with the proposition in question, and thus getting them to agree to it was hardly the point or the main point of the question. The main point was rather to frame the debate in such a way that this question and the propositional content of the answer should come to be seen as relevant to the issue being debated and thus as a premise to resolving the issue being argued over. Jackson was thus challenging his hearers to accept the idea that the length of experience that they had had of the Constitution was a relevant premise when deciding the question of whether they should consider amendments in the House of Representatives at that time. (Rudanko (2003, 56 f.))

Similarly, with the second rhetorical question, Jackson's purpose was to get the intended answer "to form a basis on which the hearers should act" (Rudanko (2003, 57)). That is, since it was difficult or impossible to identify "one proposition that is a certain and absolute amendment," the House of Representatives should not, according to Jackson's reasoning, agree to Madison's motion for discussing amendments.

To sum up this discussion of rhetorical questions, it is possible to identify two broad ways in argumentative discourse in which a speaker asking a rhetorical question may seek to affect the addressee. These may be described as follows:

Orientation towards Propositional Content. The speaker's main aim is to obtain the addressee's agreement on the propositional content of the expected answer.

Orientation towards Criteriality. The speaker's main aim is to obtain the addressee's agreement on the criteriality of the propositional content of the expected answer to resolving the issue being debated.

The two aims of the speaker, as described in (1) and (2), are not mutually exclusive. Instead, they support each other and are complementary to each other, since the aim of the speaker is to affect and to alter the beliefs and the behavior of the addressee. At the same time, it is still possible to say that for instance in the case of Jackson's first rhetorical question "What experience have we had of the good or bad qualities of the Constitution?", the emphasis is on the orientation towards criteriality.

Rhetorical questions can be an effective means of persuasion. However, in the present instance, the appeal of Jackson's speech may have been undercut by a factor to be identified in the following section.

James Jackson and *Ad Socordiam*

Jackson ended his speech as follows:

> Let the Constitution have a fair trial; let it be examined by experience, discover by that test what its errors are, and then talk of amending; but to attempt it now is doing it at a risk, which is certainly imprudent. I have the honor of coming from a State that ratified the Constitution by the unanimous vote of a numerous convention; the people of Georgia have manifested their attachment to it by adopting a State Constitution framed upon the same plan as this. But although they are thus satisfied, I shall not be against such amendments as will gratify the inhabitants of other States, provided they are judged of by experience and not merely on theory. For this reason, I wish the consideration of the subject postponed till the 1st of March, 1790. (Gales (1834, 426))

Jackson appears here to be trying to promote a posture of fair-mindedness by stating that even though his own constituents are satisfied with the Constitution and do not look for amendments, he is ready to approve them. He only asks: "let it [the Constitution, JR] be examined by experience, discover by that test what its errors are, and then talk of amending." He ended his speech by proposing that the subject be postponed by some nine months, till the following March.

Jackson's motion for a postponement, the reasons that he offered and the intention that he ostensibly had when making his motion may be analyzed in the following way:

Jackson's intention:
    Securing a postponement of the consideration of amendments.
Reasons on which the intention is based:
    It is necessary to put the Government into operation and to gain experience
    of the new Constitution before considering and approving amendments to
    the Constitution.
Proposal:
    Postpone the consideration of amendments till March 1790.

Jackson's reasoning may appear perfectly reasonable at first sight. However, the present author believes that the proposal may be, and should be, interpreted as a fallacy.[2] The term "fallacy" comes from informal logic and may be applied to "arguments that are *psychologically* persuasive but *logically* incorrect; that *do* as a matter of fact persuade but, given certain a standards, *shouldn't* (Copi and Burgess-Jackson (1996, 97), emphasis in the original).

An example of a standard fallacy is the fallacy of *ad ignorantiam,* or the appeal to ignorance. Here is an example from Douglas Walton's work: "Nobody has ever shown conclusively that ghosts do not exist; therefore we can conclude that ghosts exist" (Walton (1998a, 25)).

However, as Walton rightly emphasizes, the same kind of reasoning is not always fallacious. Here is another example: "We haven't heard from Robinson for ten years, and there has been no positive evidence, in all that time, that he is alive; therefore let us conclude that Robinson is dead" (Walton (1998a, 25)). The argument here can very well be non-fallacious, for instance, "for the purpose of settling Robinson's estate" (Walton (1998a, 25)).

It is therefore important to realize that an argument based on a certain type of reasoning may be fallacious in one context but non-fallacious in another. The following definition has been proposed by the present author, with special reference to argumentative discourse:

A fallacy is an argument or a tactic of a counter-constructive or deceptive nature used
by a speaker in an attempt to prevail over an opponent in a dialogue. (Rudanko (2003,
27))

The concept of a fallacy as espoused here is thus premised on the normative notion that in a dialogue there is a certain standard of argumentation that participants engaged in debating a course of action can reasonably be expected to meet. The counter-constructiveness of a fallacious argument, as understood here, builds on the idea of such a standard in that an argument that fails to measure up to the standard may be labeled as counter-constructive.

Two ways, in particular, can be identified in which an argument may be counter-constructive. One may be summarized as follows:

> It may simply be that an argument is a bad argument and fails to establish the conclusion. However, such an argument may still be used to cut off or to impede the proper unfolding of a dialogue. (Rudanko (2001, 53))

Secondly, counter-constructiveness may involve

> ... a deliberate intention on the part of the speaker to follow a hidden agenda and to mislead his or her interlocutors about his or her true aims and motives. ... The speaker may in this case be characterized as non-cooperative and deceptive, for a cooperative speaker can be expected to indicate the objectives that he or she has in mind when proposing a certain course of action. (Rudanko (2001, 53))

The claim is thus that an argument may be identified as fallacious on the basis of speaker intentions. This idea is found in the work of the nineteenth-century philosopher Jeremy Bentham ([1824, 1952] 1962, 129, 131). It is generally shunned in standard treatments of fallacies today. However, it is argued here is that it can have an important role to play in the analysis of political rhetoric.

More precisely, it is claimed here that Jackson was engaging in the fallacy of *ad socordiam*. This fallacy is generally not included in standard treatments of fallacies today, presumably because of the desire to avoid the notion of a speaker intention in the study of fallacies. However, it is found in Jeremy Bentham's work. He has two fallacies under this label. In his engaging style, he gives one the title of the "Procrastinator's Argument, or 'Wait a little, This is Not the Time'," and the other that of the "Snail's Pace Argument, or 'One Thing at a Time! Not too Fast! Slow and Sure!'."

He characterizes the first of these as follows:

> This is the sort of argument which we so often see employed by those who, being actually hostile to a measure, are afraid or ashamed of being seen to be so. They pretend, perhaps, to approve of the measure; they only differ as to the proper time to bring it forward. But only too often their real wish is to see it defeated forever. (Bentham ([1824, 1952] 1962, 129))

As for the second, Bentham writes:

> Suppose that there are half a dozen abuses which equally and with equal promptitude stand in need of reform. This fallacy requires, that without any assignable reason save that which is contained in the pronouncing or writing of the word "gradual," all but one or two of them shall remain untouched. Or suppose that six operations must be performed in order that some one of the abuses should be

effectually corrected. To save the reform from the reproach of being violent and intemperate, and to secure for it the praise of graduality, moderation, and temperance, you insist that, of these half-a-dozen necessary operations, some one or two only shall be talked about and proposed to be done. One of them is to be embodied in a bill to be introduced at this session if it be not too late (which you will contrive that is shall be), and another at the next session, which time being come, nothing more will be said about the matter, and there it will end. (Bentham ([1824, 1952] 1962, 131 f.))

Bentham applies the label "ad socordiam" to both of these fallacies, and the same terminology is adopted here.

Ad socordiam is well covered by Bentham's general definition of a fallacy:

BY THE NAME OF *fallacy* it is common to designate any argument employed or topic suggested for the purpose, or with the probability of producing the effect of deception, or of causing some erroneous opinion to be entertained by any person to whose mind such an argument may have been presented. (Bentham, ([1824, 1952] 1962, 3))

Bentham does not employ the term "counter-constructive," central to the definition adopted here, but his definition is covered by the term, as defined above.

It is now imperative to examine the basis of the claim that Jackson was engaging in the fallacy of *ad socordiam* when putting forward his motion. Put in a simple way, the question is whether he was putting forward his motion for a postponement of the debate by some nine months in order to get amendments approved if debated nine months later, or whether the motion was a mere pretext or an excuse meant to disguise his real intention of killing the project. The latter interpretation of his intention and tactic might be represented in the following way:

Intention (hidden):
    Thwart the project of amendments.
Reason or Rationale on which the intention is based:
    Attitude of opposition to amendments.
Tactic chosen to carry out the intention:
    Propose a postponement of the consideration of amendments till March 1790. (Cf. Rudanko (2001, 50))

At this time over two hundred years later, it is impossible to have direct access to Jackson's intentions and to make an absolutely definitive determination about them. However, it is still possible to make inferences about speaker intentions. What the speaker said is one source of evidence to draw on. However, since we are dealing with a hidden intention, the words of the speaker are not a reliable source on which to base inferences.

In the present case, it is possible to consider what followed James Jackson's speech in the debate. The member of the House of Representatives who spoke immediately after Jackson was Benjamin Goodhue. He said in part:

> Mr. GOODHUE.—I believe it would be perfectly right in the gentleman who spoke last, to move a postponement to the time he has mentioned; because he is opposed to the consideration of amendments altogether. (Gales (1834, 426))

The speaker immediately after Mr. Goodhue was Edanus Burke, who did not mention James Jackson's speech, but the member who spoke immediately after Burke was James Madison, and he began his second speech as follows:

> Mr. MADISON.—The gentleman from Georgia (Mr. JACKSON) is certainly right in his opposition to my motion for going into a Committee of the Whole, because he is unfriendly to the object I have in contemplation; ... (Gales 1834, 426 f.)

The comments by Goodhue and Madison reveal how Jackson's intentions were interpreted by two of his colleagues on June 8, 1789. Of course, there is the possibility that the intentions might have been misrepresented. To explore this question, it is useful to introduce the concept of "exigence":

> ... every intervention by one of the participants in a conversation or in a polemical exchange sets up a rhetorical exigence that the following participant must satisfy. For example, a question demands a reply, an objection, a rebuttal (or a concession). (Dascal and Gross (1999, 114))

The claim by Goodhue and Madison about Jackson's intentions — that Jackson was "opposed to the consideration of amendments altogether" — created a rhetorical exigence that demanded a rebuttal or a denial from Jackson. Failure to deny the assertion may be a legitimate basis for the inference that the claim by Goodhue and Madison was correct.

Jackson's second speech came a little later in the debate, but to make a judgment about his intentions, it seems advisable to relax the chronology of the debate slightly and to quote part of it here:

> Mr. JACKSON.—The more I consider the subject of amendments, the more I am convinced it is improper. I revere the rights of my constituents as much as any gentleman in Congress ... and that for some of the reasons referred to by the gentleman last up. If such an addition is not dangerous or improper, it is at least unnecessary; that is a sufficient reason for not entering into the subject at a time when there are urgent calls for our attention to important business. ...
>
> There are, Mr. Speaker, a number of important bills on the table which require despatch; but I am afraid, if we enter on this business, we shall not be able to attend to

them for a long time. Look, sir, over the long list of amendments proposed by some of the adopting States, and say, when the House could get through the discussion; and I believe, sir, every one of those amendments will come before us. Gentlemen may feel themselves called by duty or inclination to oppose them. How are we then to extricate ourselves from this labyrinth of business? Certainly we shall lose much of our valuable time, without any advantage whatsoever. (Gales (1834, 442, 444))

Jackson, speaking in the exigence created in part by Goodhue's and Madison's claims about his intentions, did not seek to rebut or to deny their claims. Instead, the statement "The more I consider the subject of amendments, the more I am convinced it is improper" at the beginning of the speech suggests that at that time he was among those Federalists mentioned in chapter 2 — Roger Sherman, Ralph Izard — who were opposed to amendments of any type.

In the context of the debate Goodhue's and Madison's claim about Jackson remained without a rebuttal. The identification of a hidden intention behind Jackson's motion for a nine-month postponement of the consideration of amendments may have weakened the impact of his forceful speeches in the debate.

Towards James Madison's Main Speech

In the further course of his second speech, the beginning of which was quoted above, Madison said in part:

I wish then to commence the consideration [of amendments, JR] at the present moment; I hold it to be my duty to unfold my ideas, and explain myself to the House in some form or another without delay. I only wish to introduce the great work, and, as I said before, I do not expect it will be decided immediately, but if some step is taken in the business, it will give reason to believe that we may come to a final result. This will inspire a reasonable hope in the advocates for amendments that full justice will be done to the important subject; and I have reason to believe their expectation will not be defeated. I hope the House will not decline my motion for going into a committee. (Gales (1834, 427))

Madison thus pointed out that he did not expect the consideration of amendments to be finished immediately. He was thus showing sensitivity to the views of those opposed to his motion.

The next speaker was Roger Sherman:

Mr. SHERMAN.— I am willing that this matter should be brought before the House at a proper time. I suppose a number of gentlemen think it their duty to bring it forward; so that there is no apprehension it will be passed over in silence. Other gentlemen may be disposed to let the subject rest until the more important objects of Government are attended to; and I should conclude, from the nature of the case, that the people expect the latter from us in preference to altering the Constitution; because they have ratified that instrument, in order that the Government may begin to operate. If this was not their wish, they might as well have rejected the Constitution, as North Carolina has done, until the amendments took place. The State I have the honor to come from adopted this system by a very great majority, because they wished for the Government; but they desired no amendments. I suppose this was the case in other States; it will therefore be imprudent to neglect much more important concerns for this. The executive part of the Government wants organization; the business of the revenue is incomplete, to say nothing of the judiciary business. Now, will gentlemen give up these points to go into a discussion of amendments, when no advantage can arise from them? For my part, I question if any alteration which can be now proposed would be an amendment, in the true sense of the word; but, nevertheless, I am willing to let the subject be introduced. If the gentleman only desires to go into committee for the purpose of receiving his propositions, I shall consent; but I have strong objections to being interrupted in completing the more important business; because I am well satisfied it will alarm the fears of twenty of our constituents where it will please one. (Gales (1834, 427 f.))

As noted, Roger Sherman was a Federalist who had been an opponent of amendments at the Constitutional Convention and who had not modified his opposition afterwards. He has sometimes been called an arch-foe of amendments.

In his speech Sherman made it plain that while he was willing to go into a Committee, this was for the purpose of receiving Madison's amendments only. He cited the pressure of other business as preventing the consideration of amendments, but he also made it plain that he was intrinsically opposed to them. This emerges clearly enough from statements such as "no advantage can arise from them," and that the project of amendments "will alarm the fears of twenty of our constituents where it will please one."

There is another feature of Sherman's speech, of a more subtle nature, that deserves attention. At the beginning of his speech he referred to the motives of those arguing for amendments, suggesting that they were acting from a sense of duty to bring the subject forward and to ensure that it not "be passed over in silence." Sherman used the plural, but the only speaker who had argued for amendments in a forceful way in the debate up this point had been James Madison, and it is reasonable to say that the reference was primarily to Madison, with the use of the plural being a way for Sherman to soften his statement by avoiding a direct personal reference. Sherman's statement should then be seen in the context of what may be taken to be mutually shared knowledge about the election pledge that Madison had made in the course of the election campaign for the first United States House of Representatives. As noted in chapter 2, Madison had pledged, if elected, to support amendments in the House of Representatives.

Seen against this background, Sherman's statement brings to mind a fallacy. Sherman probably had never heard of fallacy theory, but it may be suggested that he was suggesting that Madison was engaging in a fallacy when proposing amendments. The fallacy in question is a variety of the argument of *ad hominem.* The fallacy of *ad hominem,* broadly speaking, designates an attack against the person, where the substance of the point at issue becomes secondary.

The particular type of *ad hominem* that fits the present instance is the circumstantial *ad hominem.* This has been described as follows:

> The 'argumentum ad hominem,' ... is addressed to the peculiar circumstances, character, avowed opinions, or past conduct of the individual, and therefore has reference to him only, and does not bear directly and absolutely on the real question, ... (Whately, ([1827] 1975, 191))

Sherman's suggestion is that when proposing amendments, Madison was acting merely to fulfill his campaign pledge, or out of an obligation to fulfill the pledge because he had made the pledge, rather than out of a genuine commitment to the content of the measure. To put it another way, Sherman was suggesting that Madison was making a token effort, or going through the motions of proposing amendments, because he was acting merely to fulfill his campaign promise, and that such an effort was appropriate but sufficient. The concept of the circumstantial *ad hominem,* as defined by Whately, is sufficiently broad to encompass this kind of motivational *ad hominem* argument, where it is claimed that the heart of the arguer is not fully in the argument that he or she is putting forward or appears to be putting forward.

Alexander White, speaking next, was more sympathetic to the project of amendments. He said in part:

> Whether, while we are without experience, amendments can be digested in such a manner as to give satisfaction to a Constitutional majority of this House, I will not pretend to say, but I hope the subject may be considered with all convenient speed. ...
> I fear, if we refuse to take up the subject, it will irritate many of our constituents, which I do not wish to do. (Gales (1834, 428))

William Smith, of South Carolina, spoke next. Here is part of the record of his speech:

> Mr. SMITH, of South Carolina, thought the gentleman who brought forward the subject had done his duty: he had supported his motion with ability and candor, and if he did not succeed, he was not to blame. On considering what had been urged for going into a committee, he was induced to join the gentleman; but it would be merely

to receive his propositions, ... (Gales (1834, 429))

Smith was thus ready to go into a committee, but merely to receive Madison's propositions. He also took up the theme originally introduced by Roger Sherman: by introducing the subject of amendments, Madison had already done his duty, and this was sufficient. Smith was thus seeking to view Madison's efforts for amendments in the light of the fallacy of *ad hominem,* of the motivational variety.

Speaking next, John Page was the first Representative in the debate to offer genuine support and an independent argument for Madison's motion. He wanted the House to receive Madison's propositions and warned that it would be disagreeable to the people if the subject were postponed:

> Putting myself into the place of those who favor amendments, I should suspect Congress did not mean seriously to enter upon the subject; that it was in vain to expect redress from them. I should begin to turn my attention to the alternative contained in the fifth article, and think of joining the Legislatures of those States which have applied for calling a new convention. How dangerous such an expedient would be I need not mention; but I venture to affirm, that unless you take early notice of this subject, you will not have the power to deliberate. The people will clamor for a new convention; they will not trust the House any longer. Those, therefore, who dread the assembling of a convention, will do well to acquiesce in the present motion, and lay the foundation of a most important work. (Gales (1834, 429))

There was scarcely anything less palatable to Federalists at this time than the possibility or the prospect of a new Constitutional Convention, for such a convention might have diluted the powers of the Federal Government by introducing structural amendments and by thus endangering the system of the newly created Federal Government. By invoking a shared danger, Page sought to alleviate the distaste of Federalists for Madison's procedural amendments.

Speaking next, John Vining argued against Madison's motion at length. He started by voicing the worry that a consideration of amendments would disrupt the organization of the new national government:

> Mr. VINING.—I hope the House will not go into a Committee of the Whole. It strikes me that the great amendment which the Government wants is expedition in the despatch of business. The wheels of the national machine cannot turn, until the impost and collection bill are perfected; these are the desiderata which the public mind is anxiously expecting. It is well known, that all we have hitherto done amounts to nothing, if we leave the business in its present state. True; but, say gentlemen, let us go into committee; it will take but a short time; yet may it not take a considerable proportion of our time? May it not be procrastinated into days, weeks, nay, months? It is not the most facile subject that can come before the Legislature of the Union.

Gentlemen's opinions do not run parallel on this topic; it may take up more time to unite or concentre them than is now imagined. And what object is to be attained by going into a committee? If information is what we seek after, cannot that be obtained by the gentleman's laying his propositions on the table; they can be read, or they can be printed. ...

If the honorable mover of the question before the House does not think he discharges his duty without bringing his propositions forward, let him take the mode I have mentioned, ... (Gales (1834, 429 f.))

A stylistic feature favored by Vining is the rhetorical question. Here we might recall the rhetorical questions used by another of Madison's opponents, James Jackson, as discussed above. In that discussion, a distinction was made between rhetorical questions oriented towards obtaining audience agreement on propositional content and those oriented towards obtaining audience agreement on criteriality, and it was observed that Jackson's rhetorical questions tended to have an orientation towards obtaining criteriality. Vining's rhetorical questions, for their part, tend to have an orientation towards the propositional content of the expected answer. For instance, consider "... may it not take a considerable proportion of our time?" and "May it not be procrastinated into days, weeks, nay, months?" The expected answers are of the type "It surely may take a considerable proportion of our time" and "It surely may be procrastinated into days, weeks, months." In the case of these rhetorical questions, if the audience had accepted the propositional content of the expected answers, that the consideration of amendments would take months, it is hard to imagine that Madison's motion would have survived. In any event, the importance of the content of these answers to the question of whether to accede to Madison's motion was obvious.

He ended his speech as follows:

> ... I wish to see every proposition which comes from that worthy gentleman on the science of Government, but I think it can be presented better by staying where we are, than going into committee, and therefore shall vote against his motion. (Gales (1834, 431))

James Madison's Main Speech

Following John Vining, James Madison spoke for the third time. He started by offering an apology and by modifying his original proposal for going into a Committee of the Whole:

> Mr. MADISON.—I am sorry to be accessory to the loss of a single moment of time by the House. If I had been indulged in my motion, and we had gone into a Committee of

the Whole, I think we might have rose and resumed the consideration of other business before this time; that is, so far as it depended upon what I proposed to bring forward. As that mode seems not to give satisfaction, I will withdraw the motion, and move you, sir, that a select committee be appointed to consider and report such amendments as are proper for Congress to propose to the Legislatures of the several States, conformably to the fifth article of the Constitution. (Gales (1834, 431))

In thus modifying his proposal, Madison was being flexible in response to the rhetorical exigence set up by the speeches in the debate so far.

In the next part of his speech Madison identified his reasons for proposing amendments. He started by freely acknowledging that he felt himself to be bound by a duty to propose amendments:

If I thought I could fulfil the duty which I owe to myself and my constituents, to let the subject pass over in silence, I most certainly should not trespass upon the indulgence of this House. But I cannot do this, and am therefore compelled to beg a patient hearing to what I have to lay before you. (Gales (1834, 431))

By using words indicating his reluctance to impose on his audience, as in "**compelled** to **beg** a **patient** hearing to what I **have to** lay before you," Madison signaled his sensitivity to their face wants.

He then moved to the substantive reasons that motivated him to propose amendments at this time, so early in the life of the new Republic. Here is one of his arguments:

It cannot be a secret to the gentlemen in this House, that, notwithstanding the ratification of this system of Government by eleven of the thirteen United States, in some cases unanimously, in others by large majorities; yet still there is a great number of our constituents who are dissatisfied with it; among whom are many respectable for their talents and patriotism and respectable for the jealousy they have for their liberty, which, though mistaken in its object, is laudable in its motive. There is a great body of the people falling under this description, who at present feel much inclined to join their support to the cause of Federalism, if they were satisfied on this one point. We ought not to disregard their inclination, but, on principles of amity and moderation, conform to their wishes, and expressly declare the great rights of mankind secured under this Constitution. The acquiescence which our fellow-citizens show under the Government, calls upon us for a like return of moderation. (Gales (1834, 432))

Here Madison used his position as a prominent Federalist to appeal to his fellow Federalists to show moderation and a spirit of conciliation towards those who were not Federalists but might give their more wholehearted support to the new Government if amendments were added to the new Constitution.

Madison then proceeded to another consideration, even more important in his mind, that also related to satisfying those who had been skeptical of the new Constitution:

> But perhaps there is a stronger motive than this for our going into a consideration of the subject. It is to provide those securities for liberty which are required by a part of the community; I allude in a particular manner to those two States that have not thought fit to throw themselves into the bosom of the Confederacy. It is a desirable thing, on our part as well as theirs, that a re-union should take place as soon as possible. I have no doubt, if we proceed to take those steps which would be prudent and requisite at this juncture, that in a short time we should see that disposition prevailing in those States which have not come in, that we have seen prevailing in those States which have embraced the Constitution. (Gales (1834, 432))

The two States in question were North Carolina and Rhode Island, and Madison again appealed to his fellow Federalists that amendments would make the Union whole again, knowing that Federalists were hardly likely to wish to weaken the new Republic by the "loss" of two States.

Madison then turned to the content of the project of amendments:

> But I will candidly acknowledge, that, over and above all these considerations, I do conceive that the Constitution may be amended; that is to say, if all power is subject to abuse, that then it is possible the abuse of the powers of the General Government may be guarded against in a more secure manner than is now done, while no one advantage arising from the exercise of that power shall be damaged or endangered by it. We have in this way something to gain, and, if we proceed with caution, nothing to lose. And in this case it is necessary to proceed with caution; for while we feel all these inducements to go into a revisal of the Constitution, we must feel for the Constitution itself, and make that revisal a moderate one. I should be unwilling to see a door opened for a reconsideration of the whole structure of the Government—for a re-consideration of the principles and the substance of the powers given; because I doubt, if such a door were opened, we should be very likely to stop at that point which would be safe to the Government itself. But I do wish to see a door opened to consider, so far as to incorporate those provisions for the security of rights against which I believe no serious objection has been made by any class of our constituents; such as would be likely to meet with the concurrence of two-thirds of the State Legislatures. (Gales (1834, 432 f.))

Madison's argument here concerned the intrinsic content of amendments: he wanted them in order to guard against "the abuse of the powers of the General Government." Madison's commitment to amendments thus went beyond a desire to make the new Constitution more palatable to those who were skeptical towards it without amendments. Amendments, in his view, were inherently desirable.

At the same time, Madison took great care to reassure his Federalist colleagues that he was opposed to permitting a reconsideration of the structure of the new government. Using the terms introduced above — admittedly, these terms come from later analysis and were not Madison's — he made it clear that he was opposed to structural amendments and that the consideration of amendments would only involve rights-related or procedural amendments.

In the further course of the speech, Madison proceeded to outline his proposals for amendments. These cannot be reviewed here in their entirety, but three proposals deserve to be mentioned. Here is his original proposal for safeguarding freedom of speech:

> The people shall not be deprived or abridged of their right to speak, to write or to publish their sentiments; and the freedom of the press, as one of the great bulwarks of liberty, shall be inviolable. (Gales (1834, 434))

In addition, Madison made a revolutionary proposal designed to ensure that States cannot limit freedom of the press. He proposed the following:

> No State shall violate the equal rights of conscience, or the freedom of the press, or the trial by jury in criminal cases. (Gales (1834, 435))

And in order to ensure that the enumeration of certain powers as being outside of the jurisdiction of the Federal and State governments should not be taken to mean that all other powers were within that jurisdiction, Madison proposed the following provision:

> The exceptions here or elsewhere in the Constitution, made in favor of particular rights, shall not be so construed as to diminish the just importance of other rights retained by the people, or as to enlarge the powers delegated by the Constitution; but either as actual limitations of such powers, or as inserted merely for greater caution. (Gales (1834, 435))

After presenting his amendments, Madison went on to further comment on some of his proposals. He did not provide a definition of his view of what freedom of the press meant, and it has sometimes been asserted that he meant the Blackstonian view of it, current in Great Britain at the time, essentially to the effect that the concept only meant the absence of censorship prior to publication, nothing more.

However, it is a dubious speculation to suggest that Madison had a Blackstonian view of freedom of the press in mind when he argued for amendments on June 8, 1789. It is important to see his failure to define his concept of freedom of the press in the context of the debate. He was presenting his proposals in the face of determined Federalist opposition to their early consideration and his main aim was to get the project of amendments off the ground. Seen against this background, his failure to discourse on the concept is natural. (On the question of Madison's original intent, see further the discussion in Rudanko (2003, 95 ff.) and the last chapter of this volume.)

It should be added that at a subsequent point in the speech he pointed to a clear distinction between practices in Great Britain and the United States:

> In the declaration of rights which that country [Great Britain, JR] has established, the truth is, they have gone no farther than to raise a barrier against the power of the Crown; the power of the Legislature is left altogether indefinite. Although I know whenever the great rights, the trial by jury, freedom of the press, or liberty of conscience, come in question in that body, the invasion of them is resisted by able advocates, yet their Magna Charta does not contain any one provision for the security of those rights, respecting which the people of America are most alarmed. The freedom of the press and rights of conscience, those choicest privileges of the people, are unguarded in the British Constitution.
>
> But although the case may be widely different, and it may not be thought necessary to provide limits for the legislative power in that country, yet a different opinion prevails in the United States. The people of many States have thought it necessary to raise barriers against power in all forms and departments of Government, and I am inclined to believe, if once bills of rights are established in all the States as well as the Federal Constitution, we shall find, that, although some of them are rather unimportant, yet, upon the whole, they will have a salutary tendency. (Gales (1834, 436))

Madison was thus arguing that his proposals went beyond British provisions regarding the safeguarding of freedom of the press, and that it was necessary to guard against legislative intrusion. In other words, Madison's purpose here was to establish that even though it had not been done in Great Britain, it was necessary to safeguard freedom of the press against legislative intrusion.

Madison then focused on the question as to whose powers the amendments were meant to restrain:

> ... the great object in view is to limit and qualify the powers of Government, by excepting out of the grant of power those cases in which the Government ought not to act, or to act only in a particular mode. They point these exceptions sometimes against the abuse of the Executive power, sometimes against the Legislative, and, in some cases, against the community itself; or, in other words, against the majority in favor of the minority. (Gales (1834, 437))

Here is how Madison developed his point about protecting a minority within a community:

> It may be thought that all paper barriers against the power of the community are too weak to be worthy of attention. I am sensible they are not so strong as to satisfy gentlemen of every description who have seen and examined thoroughly the texture of such a defence; yet, as they have a tendency to impress some degree of respect for them, to establish the public opinion in their favor, and rouse the attention of the whole community, it may be one means to control the majority from those acts to which they might be otherwise inclined. (Gales, (1834, 437))

In the further course of his remarks Madison addressed a number of objections that had been raised to a Bill of Rights. For instance, he argued as follows:

> It has been said, that in the Federal Government they [provisions of a Bill of Rights, JR] are unnecessary, because the powers are enumerated, and it follows, that all that are not granted by the Constitution are retained; that the Constitution is a bill of powers, the great residuum being the rights of the people; and, therefore, a bill of rights cannot be so necessary as if the residuum were thrown into the hands of the Government. I admit that these arguments are not entirely without foundation; but they are not conclusive to the extent which has been supposed. It is true, the powers of the General Government are circumscribed, they are directed to particular objects; but even if Government keeps within those limits, it has certain discretionary powers with respect to the means, which may admit of abuse to a certain extent, in the same manner as the powers of the State Governments under their constitutions may to an indefinite extent; because in the Constitution of the United States, there is a clause granting to Congress the power to make all laws which shall be necessary and proper for carrying into execution all the powers vested in the Government of the United States, ... Now, may not laws be considered necessary and proper by Congress (for it is for them to judge of the necessity and propriety to accomplish those special purposes, which they may have in contemplation,) which laws in themselves are neither necessary nor proper, as well as improper laws could be enacted by the State Legislatures, for fulfilling the more extended objects of those Governments? (Gales (1834, 438))

Rhetorical questions were very rare in Madison's rhetoric on June 8, 1789, but here he used one. It is of the content-oriented variety.

As regards substance, Madison's argument reveals a down-to-earth sense of realism about laws that may be enacted by Congress and a desire to guard the rights of the people against encroachment by government.

Further, he dealt with the objection that the enumeration of certain rights might "disparage those rights not placed in that enumeration" (Gales (1834, 439)). In response he pointed to his provision, quoted above, guarding against such a misinterpretation.

As for the argument that bills of rights had not been effective at the State level:

> It has been said that it is unnecessary to load the Constitution with this provision, because it was not found effectual in the constitution of particular States. It is true, there are a few particular States in which some of the most valuable articles have not, at one time of other, been violated; but it does not follow but they may have, to a certain degree, a salutary effect against the abuse of power. If they are incorporated into the Constitution, independent tribunals of justice will consider themselves in a peculiar manner the guardians of those rights; ... (Gales (1834, 439))

Towards the end of his speech Madison reassured his fellow Federalists in this way:

> ... I believe every gentleman will readily admit that nothing is in contemplation, so far as I have mentioned, that can endanger the beauty of the Government in any one important feature, even in the eyes of its most sanguine admirers. I have proposed nothing that does not appear to me as proper in itself, or eligible as patronized by a respectable number of our fellow-citizens; and if we can make the Constitution better in the opinion of those who are opposed to it, without weakening its frame, or abridging its usefulness in the judgment of those who are attached to it, we act the part of wise and liberal men to make such alterations as shall produce that effect. (Gales (1834, 441))

At the very end of his speech, Madison repeated his motion that a select committee be appointed to consider amendments:

> ... I shall content myself, for the present, with moving "that a committee be appointed to consider of and report such amendments as ought to be proposed by Congress to the Legislatures of the States, to become, if ratified by three-fourths thereof, part of the Constitution of the United States." By agreeing to this motion, the subject may be going on in committee, while other important business is proceeding to a conclusion in the House. I should advocate greater despatch in the business of amendments, if I were not convinced of the absolute necessity there is of pursuing the organization of the Government; because I think we should obtain the confidence of our fellow-citizens, in proportion as we fortify the rights of the people against the encroachments of the Government. (Gales (1834, 442))

Madison thus provided further reassurance to his fellow Federalists, by arguing that while the business of amendments was being considered by a committee, the House would be able to attend to other business.

After Madison's Major Speech

James Jackson's second speech, already referred to above, came immediately after Madison's major speech. As regards the Federalist Jackson, Madison's reassurances failed, for Jackson started his speech by saying that "The more I consider the business of amendments, the more I am convinced it is improper."

In the further course of his speech Jackson argued that there was no reason for the suspicions that a Bill of Rights was designed to remove. He also warned that if they entered on discussing amendments now, they would need to do so again after Rhode Island and North Carolina had joined the Union:

> But to return to my argument. It being the case that those States are not yet come into the Union, when they join us, we shall have another list of amendments to consider, and another bill of rights to frame. (Gales (1834, 443))

In the absence of an argument showing that those in Rhode Island and North Carolina wanted a substantially different kind of a Bill of Rights, Jackson's argument here may be considered a pre-text for opposing Madison's motion. It may be viewed as another type of *ad socordiam.*

Jackson went on as follows, discussing what he took to be the dilemma that the country would place itself in if the House started to consider amendments:

> But in what situation shall we be with respect to those foreign Powers with whom we desire to be in treaty? They look upon us as a nation emerging into figure and importance. But what will be their opinion, if they see us unable to retain the national advantages we have just gained? They will smile at our infantine efforts to obtain consequence, and treat us with the contempt we have hitherto borne by reason of the imbecility of our Government. Can we expect to enter into a commercial competition with any of them, while our system is incomplete? And how long will it remain in such a situation, if we enter upon amendments, God only knows. Our instability will make us objects of scorn. We are not content with two revolutions in less than fourteen years; we must enter upon a third, without necessity or propriety. (Gales (1834, 443))

Jackson's initial rhetorical question has some orientation toward criteriality, for he is arguing that members of the House of Representatives should pay attention to the view that foreign powers take of the discussion of amendments as they decide whether or not to debate amendments. At the same time, there is a degree of a propositional orientation and the expected answer is less obvious than in some other rhetorical questions, It should be added that the rhetorical question also serves to introduce a new topic into his argument, illustrating the topic shifting function that rhetorical questions sometimes have.

Substantively, Jackson engages in some name-calling here, by using the word *infantine* to characterize how the nation would be perceived if the House entered on a discussion of amendments. The use of such an emotionally charged word, designed to disparage the opposing side, involves a fallacy. By ridiculing a proposal with an emotional epithet, the speaker distracts attention from its content. The use of the emotional epithet is thus an instance of the fallacy of begging the question. This fallacy "involves the essential use of circular argumentation that, while not fallacious in itself, is fallaciously used to evade a proper fulfillment of burden of proof in a dialogue" (Walton (1995, 12)).

Jackson concluded his speech as follows:

> There are, Mr. Speaker, a number of important bills on the table which require despatch; but I am afraid, if we enter on this business, we shall not be able to attend to them for a long time. Look, sir, over the long list of amendments proposed by some of the adopting States, and say, when the House could get through the discussion; and I believe, sir, every one of those amendments will come before us. Gentlemen may feel themselves called by duty or inclination to oppose them. How are we to extricate ourselves from this labyrinth of business? Certainly we shall lose much of our valuable time, without any advantage whatsoever. I hope, therefore, the gentleman will press us no further; he has done his duty, and acquitted himself of the obligation under which he lay. He may now accede to what I take to be the sense of the House, and let the business of amendments lie over till next Spring; that will be soon enough to take it up to any good purpose. (Gales (1834, 444))

Jackson thus returned to the fallacy of motivational *ad hominem,* originally inserted into the debate by Roger Sherman, by suggesting that Madison had done his duty by making an attempt to introduce amendments and thereby fulfilled the promise that he had given as part of his election campaign, with the fate and content of amendments becoming a secondary issue.

What was perhaps more remarkable than Jackson's use of the motivational *ad hominem* was the assurance with which he used it: he felt confident enough to speak of "the sense of the House" as being against Madison's motion.

Elbridge Gerry, an Antifederalist, spoke next. In the early part of his speech he argued that the consideration of amendments should be postponed, but only by a short time. However, his main concern was to oppose Madison's motion for the appointment of a special committee:

> I am against referring the subject to a select committee, because I conceive it would be disrespectful to those States which have proposed amendments. The conventions of the States consisted of the most wise and virtuous men of the community; they have ratified this Constitution, in full confidence that their objections would at least

be considered; and shall we, sir, preclude them by the appointment of a special committee, to consider of a few propositions brought forward by an individual gentleman? (Gales (1834, 446))

Later in his speech Gerry said that he would say "nothing respecting the amendments themselves." However, what motivated his rhetorical question — expecting an answer of the type 'surely we should not preclude the proposals of State conventions from being considered — in the extract quoted was the Antifederalist concern that the amendment process would stop at procedural amendments and that no structural amendments would be approved or even considered. The concern was fully justified since Madison pointed out repeatedly that his proposals were limited to procedural amendments.

Samuel Livermore, speaking next, voiced support for amendments "at a proper time," but left no doubt about his opposition to the early consideration of amendments. He also made this point:

He wished the concurrence of the Senate upon entering on this business, because if they opposed the measure, all the House did would be mere waste of time; and there was some little difficulty on this point, because it required the consent of two-thirds of both Houses to agree to what was proper on this occasion. (Gales (1834, 447))

Livermore's argument here is potentially fallacious. If a body debating whether to debate a measure decides not to debate it until another body has pronounced on it, it deprives itself of the power to initiate the measure, and it may be that the other body will decide against debating the measure, since the first body had decided against taking the initiative. At best the procedure involves delay, and at worst, the sentiments of the first body are never ascertained regarding the content of the measure. The fallacy in question might be called the fallacy of 'wasted effort' and it is a type of procedural *ad socordiam.* Whether thwarting the measure was Livermore's intention is difficult to ascertain form his brief remarks, and the case for invoking *ad socordiam* is not fully made.

Roger Sherman, well known for his opposition to amendments, called into question the whole idea of amending the Constitution:

... amidst all the members from the twelve States present at the Federal Convention, there were only three who did not sign the instrument to attest their opinion of its goodness. Of the eleven States who have received it, the majority have ratified it without proposing a single amendment. This circumstance leads me to suppose that we shall not be able to propose any alterations that are likely to be adopted by nine States; and gentlemen know, before the alterations take effect, they must be agreed to by the Legislatures of three-fourths of the States in the Union. Those States which have not recommended alterations, will hardly adopt them, unless it is clear that they tend to make the Constitution better. Now, how this can be made out to their satisfaction I am yet to learn; they know of no defect from experience. (Gales (1834, 448))

Given Sherman's long-standing opposition to amendments, his argument here may be seen in the aspect of another type of the fallacy of wasted effort or procedural *ad socordiam*: while he did not make the consideration of amendments dependent on the prior agreement of some other body, he was saying that the chances of amendments being ratified were so slim that they would have been wasting their time if they had decided to debate amendments. The argument was not addressed to the content of the proposed measure, and if the rhetorical maneuver had been successful, the true sentiments of the House of Representatives regarding the content of the measure would never have been tested. Nor of course would it ever have been determined whether the requisite number of States might have ratified amendments. It is thus reasonable to regard his maneuver as a fallacy.

His opposition to amendments is confirmed by what he said next in the present speech:

> It seems to be the opinion of gentlemen generally that this is not the time for entering upon the discussion of amendments: our only question therefore is, how to get rid of the subject. (Gales (1834, 448))

The sense of self-confidence with which Sherman spoke echoes Jackson's tone and reveals how precarious the fate of the Madisonian project of amendments was in the debate of June 8, 1789.

Elbridge Gerry, speaking next, is recorded as proposing a postponement of the measure till July 1, 1789, without further argument.

Thomas Sumter echoed Gerry in asking for a short delay, and he also stressed that the matter of amendments should be considered by the full House, rather than by a select committee.

John Vining, speaking next, said in part:

> ... he was doubly bound to object to amendments which were either improper or unnecessary. But he had good reasons for opposing the consideration of even proper alterations at this time. He would ask the gentleman who pressed them, whether he would be responsible to the risk the Government would run of being injured by an *interregnum*? Proposing amendments at this time, is suspending the operations of Government, and may be productive of its ruin. (Gales (1834, 449))

After this rather *ad hominem* remark directed at Madison, Vining went on to say:

There were many things mentioned by some of the State Conventions which he would never agree to, on any conditions whatever; they changed the principles of the Government, and were therefore obnoxious to its friends. The honorable gentleman from Virginia had not touched upon any of them; he was glad of it, because he could by no means bear the idea of an alteration respecting them; he referred to the mode of obtaining direct taxes, judging of elections &c. (Gales (1834, 449))

Vining's statement shows how Madison's sensitivity to Federalist concerns, and especially to Federalist opposition to structural amendments, had made an impression on Vining.

Following Vining's speech the record shows that a number of members still spoke, but reports of their remarks are brief in the record of Gales (1834). According to that record, Madison, speaking next, "moved the propositions by way of resolutions to be adopted by the House" (Gales (1834, 449)). This motion was objected to by Samuel Livermore (Gales (1834, 449)), upon which John Page asked "what was to be done when the House would not refer it [the subject of amendments, J.R.] to a committee of any sort" (Gales (1834, 450)).

After Page's remarks, John Lawrence, supported by Richard Lee, "moved to refer Mr. Madison's motion to the Committee of the Whole on the State of the Union" (Gales (1834, 450)). "At length Mr. Lawrence's motion was agreed to, and Mr. Madison's propositions were ordered to be referred to a Committee of the Whole. Adjourned." (Gales (1834, 450))

Summing Up

This investigation of the debate of June 8, 1789 has shown how precariously the fate of the Bill of Rights hung in the balance on that day. There were Federalist members present who wanted to kill the project, presumably once and for all. As Roger Sherman tellingly remarked in his second speech, "the only question now is how to get rid of the subject" (Gales 1834, 448)).

James Jackson was another Federalist who was out to kill the project, it is argued here. He ostensibly only proposed to postpone any consideration of the subject till March 1790, but there is credible evidence, based in part on the perception of his motion by his fellow members of the House of Representatives, that his true aim was to kill the project. As a consequence, it is claimed here, the fallacy of *ad socordiam* may be applied to his argument for a postponement of the consideration of amendments.

There is little doubt in the light of the present study that the project of a Bill of Rights was able to survive on June 8, 1789 only because of James Madison. Two aspects of his role are highlighted in this investigation. They both relate to Madison's person, but they may still be kept apart for the sake of discussion. First, it is clear from the debate that Federalists held Madison in high regard at that time. An indication of this is the respectful way in which they tended to refer to him. The study shows that members of the first House of Representatives tended to refer to each other with the word "gentleman," which was supplemented with an identifying modifier. For instance, here are two references to James Jackson that were included in the extracts above:

"the gentleman who spoke last" — Benjamin Goodhue referring to James Jackson
"the gentleman from Georgia" — James Madison referring to James Jackson

Some members referred to Madison in the same way but examining the two speeches of the Federalist John Vining, who was one of Madison's opponents in the debate, we find a number of epithets that testify to the respect in which Madison was held even by a member who was skeptical of the project:

the honorable mover of the question before the House
that worthy gentleman
the gentleman who pressed them [alterations, J.R.]
the honorable gentleman from Virginia

Roger Sherman, for his part, tended to avoid referring to Madison as an individual. As noted, in his first speech he used to plural, "a number of gentlemen who bring it [the matter of amendments, J.R.] forward," which was a respectful way of referring to Madison, since by that point in the debate Madison had been the only speaker arguing for amendments.

The other aspect of Madison's role emphasized by this investigation is the extraordinary dedication and perseverance with which he pursued the matter of amendments, under adverse circumstances. A frequent tactic of his Federalist colleagues was to point out that it was reasonable for him to bring up the business of amendments, in order to do his duty. They did not spell it out, but it can be presumed that they were mindful of Madison's election pledge in Virginia. The theme was first introduced by Sherman in his first speech, but it was James Jackson who voiced this argument in the most explicit way, when he said in his second speech: "I hope ... the gentleman will press us no further; he has done his duty, and acquitted himself of the obligation under which he lay" (Gales (1834, 444)).

The technique can be seen in the light of the fallacy of motivational *ad hominem*: James Jackson was suggesting that Madison was only acting in order to fulfill a promise, implying that a token effort, or an effort less than whole-hearted, for amendments was sufficient and appropriate. As Jackson went on: "He may now accede to what I take to be the sense of the House, and let the business of amendments lie over until next Spring" (Gales (1834, 444)).

Given Jackson's hostility to amendments, the analyst might silently add "when it shall be forgotten" to Jackson's statement.

However, Madison's perseverance proved that there was nothing token about his efforts and that he was thoroughly committed to bringing the business of amendments forward in a timely fashion. At no point did he agree to let the subject lie over indefinitely or till the following spring.

At the same time, he showed his sensitivity to Federalist concerns in a number of ways. He emphasized repeatedly that he was aware of the pressure of other business. And he also modified his original proposal that the House should consider amendments as a Committee of the Whole, and proposed a select committee instead.

He was also careful to stress that his amendments were all procedural and not structural. Further, he maintained a courteous tone throughout towards his Federalist colleagues, even in the face of their continuing opposition.

James Jackson was not impressed by Madison's speeches. However, the discussion suggests that John Vining was a Federalist on whom Madison's approach had an effect. Madison's sensitivity to the concerns of Federalists and his moderation may well have saved the project of amendments on June 8, 1789.

Notes to Chapter 3

1. There are two aspects to the notion of face. A succinct explanation is found in Brown and Levinson's standard work on politeness:

... all competent adult members of a society [note omitted, JR] have (and know each other to have) ... 'face', the public self-image that every member wants to claim for himself, consisting in two related aspects:

(a) negative face; [note omitted, JR] the basic claim to territories, personal preserves, rights to non-distraction — freedom of action and freedom from imposition

(b) positive face: the positive consistent self-image or 'personality' (crucially including the desire that this self-image be appreciated and approved of) claimed by interactants. (Brown and Levinson (1987, 61))

2. More precisely, the type of fallacy in question is an informal fallacy, as opposed to a formal fallacy, but formal fallacies, which can be identified "merely by examining the form (hence the name) or the structure of the argument" (Copi and Burgess-Jackson (1996, 97)), can be set aside in the present context.

Appendix

Here is the record of James Jackson's first speech:

Mr. JACKSON.—I am of opinion we ought not to be in a hurry with respect to altering the Constitution. For my part, I have no idea of speculating in this serious manner on theory. If I agree to alterations in the mode of administering this Government, I shall like to stand on the sure ground of experience, and not be treading air. What experience have we had of the good or bad qualities of this Constitution? Can any gentleman affirm to me one proposition that is a certain and absolute amendment? I deny that he can. Our Constitution, sir, is like a vessel just launched, and lying at the wharf; she is untried, you can hardly discover any one of her properties. It is not known how she will answer her helm, or lay her course; whether she will bear with safety the precious freight to be deposited in her hold. But, in this state will the prudent merchant attempt alterations? Will he employ workmen to tear off the planking and take asunder the frame? He certainly will not. Let us, gentlemen, fit out our vessel, set up her masts and expand her sails, and be guided by the experiment in our alterations. If she sails upon an uneven keel, let us right her by adding weight where it is wanting. In this way, we may remedy her defects to the satisfaction of all concerned; but if we proceed now to make alterations, we may deface a beauty or deform a well proportioned piece of workmanship. In short, Mr. Speaker, I am not for amendments at this time; but if gentlemen should think it a subject deserving of attention, they will surely not neglect the more important business which is now unfinished before them. Without we pass the collection bill we can get no revenue, and without revenue the wheels of Government cannot move. I am against taking up the subject at present, and shall therefore be totally against the amendments, if the Government is not organized, that I may see whether it is grievous or not.

When the propriety of making amendments shall be obvious from experience, I trust there will be virtue enough in my country to make them. Much has been said by the opponents to this Constitution, respecting the insecurity of jury trials, that great bulwark of personal safety. All their objections may be done away, by proper regulations on this point, and I do not fear but such regulations will take place. The bill is now before the Senate, and a proper attention is shown to this business. Indeed, I cannot conceive how it could be opposed; I think an almost omnipotent Emperor would not be hardy enough to set himself against it. Then why should we fear a power which cannot be improperly exercised?

We have proceeded to make some regulations under the Constitution; but have met with no inaccurace, unless it may be said that the clause respecting vessels bound to or from one State be obliged to enter, clear, or pay duties in another, is somewhat obscure; yet that is not sufficient, I trust, in any gentleman's opinion to induce an amendment. But let me ask what will be the consequence of taking up this subject? Are we going to finish it in an hour? I believe not; it will take us more than a day, a week, a month—it will take a year to complete it! And will it be doing our duty to our country, to neglect or delay putting the Government in motion, when every thing depends upon its being speedily done?

Let the Constitution have a fair trial; let it be examined by experience, discover by that test what its errors are, and then talk of amending; but to attempt it now is doing it at a risk, which is certainly imprudent. I have the honor of coming from a State that ratified the Constitution by the unanimous vote of a numerous convention: the people of Georgia have manifested their attachment to it, by adopting a State Constitution framed upon the same plan as this. But although they are thus satisfied, I shall not be against such amendments as will gratify the inhabitants of other States, provided they are judged of by experience and not merely on theory. For this reason, I wish the consideration of the subject postponed until the 1st of March, 1790. (Gales (1834, 425 f.))

Chapter 4
The Debate of July 21, 1789

The Dynamics of the Debate of July 21, 1789

The House of Representatives went on record in favor of considering Madison's amendments in a Committee of the Whole at the end of the debate of June 8, 1789. Several weeks passed after that date without any further action in this matter on the part of the House. However, on Tuesday, July 21, 1789 James Madison became active again. Here is the record of what he did:

> Mr. MADISON begged the House to indulge him in the further consideration of amendments to the Constitution, and as there appeared, in some degree, a moment of leisure, he would move to go into a Committee of the Whole on the subject, conformably to the order of the 8th of last month. (Gales 1834, 660))

Madison's motion was immediately answered by a countermotion from Fisher Ames, a prominent Massachusetts Federalist:

> Mr. AMES hoped that the House would be induced, on mature reflection, to rescind their vote of going into a committee on the business, and refer it to a select committee. It would certainly tend to facilitate the business. If they had the subject at large before a Committee of the Whole, he could not see where it was likely to end. The amendments proposed were so various, that their discussion must inevitably occupy many days, and that at a time when they can be ill spared; whereas a select committee could go through and cull out those of the most material kind, without interrupting the principal business of the House. He therefore moved, that the Committee of the Whole be discharged, and the subject referred to a select committee. (Gales (1834, 660))

The next speaker was Theodore Sedgwick, another Massachusetts Federalist. Here is part of the record:

> Mr. SEDGWICK opposed the motion, for the reasons given by his colleague, observing that the members from the several States proposing amendments would, no doubt, drag the House through the consideration of every one, whatever their fate

might be after they were discussed; ... (Gales (1834, 660))

Presumably, Sedgwick was opposing Madison's motion and siding with Ames. After Alexander White had voiced doubts about whether any time would be saved by appointing a select committee, Roger Sherman took the floor:

> Mr. SHERMAN.—The provision for amendments made in the fifth article of the Constitution, was intended to facilitate the adoption of those which experience should point out to be necessary. This Constitution has been adopted by eleven States; a majority of those eleven have received it without expressing a wish for amendments; now, is it probable that three-fourths of the eleven States will agree to amendments offered on mere speculative points, when the Constitution has had no kind of trial whatever? It is hardly to be expected that they will. Consequently we shall lose our labor, and had better decline having any thing further to do with it for the present.
>
> But if the House are to go into a consideration, it had better be done in such a way as not to interfere much with the organization of the Government. (Gales (1834, 661))

Sherman thus repeated his opposition to a Bill of Rights. The argument was again an appeal to the prospect of a later stage in the amendment process not succeeding, and as in chapter 3, it can be seen in the light of the fallacy of "wasted effort," a type of procedural *ad socordiam*.

John Page, who had been one of Madison few supporters on June 8, 1789, expressed a preference for not changing the earlier decision, while George Partridge, speaking next, voiced support for a select committee.

James Jackson, so active on June 8, 1789, contented himself with brief remarks now, according to the record:

> Mr. JACKSON was sorry to see the House was to be troubled any further on the subject; he looked upon it as a mere waste of time; but as he always chose the least of two evils, he acquiesced in the motion for referring it to a special committee. (Gales (1834, 661))

The next substantive contribution came from Elbridge Gerry. As in the previous debate, he voiced fears that a select committee might neglect amendments proposed by some States and argued in favor of not changing the earlier vote of going into a Committee of the Whole on the subject. However, he also argued that it was not the time to do so yet but did not specify what the appropriate time might be.

Fisher Ames, speaking next, cautioned against too much zeal in debating rights and liberties, and suggested that a select committee would be more appropriate from this point of view. He also reminded members that two thirds of both Houses would need to agree on amendments.

Thomas Tucker was strongly opposed to transferring the matter to a select committee. The following statement by this Antifederalist deserves attention here:

> The select committee will have it in their power so to keep this business back, that it may never again come before this House; this is an imprudent step for us to take; not that I would insinuate it is an event likely to take place, or which any gentleman has in contemplation. I give every gentleman credit of his declaration, and believe the honorable mover means to save time by this arrangement; but do not let us differ on this point. (Gales (1834, 664))

Tucker thus voiced a fear relating to speaker intentions: maybe the motion to refer the matter to a select committee was a ploy to bury the matter in that committee. Such a ploy brings to mind what is here called a fallacy: if Tucker's suggestion was — or had been — correct, Ames would have been engaging in a fallacy when making his motion. The fallacy in question might be called "kill in committee," and it can be viewed as another type of a procedural *ad socordiam.*

Tucker disavowed this interpretation of Ames's motion immediately, but the fact that he voiced it is worth noting, indicating the sensitivity of speakers in the debate to potential ploys or fallacies.

Elbridge Gerry, speaking next, again opposed a select committee. Again he voiced his fear that the House would be restricted in its consideration of the subject by the report of the Committee.

After Gerry's speech, the House of Representatives divided, with Ames's motion prevailing. A select committee was set up. Its members included Madison, Sherman, Vining and Goodhue, but neither Gerry nor Ames.

Assessing the Debate of July 21, 1789

The debate of July 21, 1789 is not a well-known event in the history of the Bill of Rights. To judge by the evidence in Gales (1834), the speeches in this debate tended to be much shorter than in the first procedural debate of June 8, 1789.

However, the debate still had significance. One important question concerns Fisher Ames's motive when making his proposal. If his intention was indeed to kill the project of amendments, by burying it in a committee, his proposal for a select committee was a fallacy. As noted, the possibility of such an interpretation was voiced by Representative Tucker.

In the view of the present author, Ames was not engaging in a fallacy and was not being disingenuous when making his proposal. He was a Federalist, but he had voiced support for amendments in his election campaign. More significantly, if his motion had been perceived to be a ploy to bury the matter in a committee, it might have been expected that James Madison would have taken a more active part in the debate. Madison started the debate, but after his initial speech he did not speak again. Most significantly, he did not oppose Ames's motion. This suggests that he was ready to have it pass and ready to give it his silent blessing.

The hypothesis that Madison was ready to give his silent blessing to Ames's motion receives further support from the fact that in the debate of June 8, 1789 Madison himself proposed a select committee as the way forward. It is recalled that this was one of the ways in which he had sought to make the project of amendments less disagreeable to Federalists.

With the benefit of hindsight it is safe to say that by moving the appointment of a select committee, Fisher Ames did a major service for the project of amendments. It should be recalled that Federalists had a large majority in the first House of Representatives. As seen in the debate, there were Federalists, including Roger Sherman, who continued to oppose the consideration of amendments or to feel hesitant or ambivalent about the project. A free-wheeling debate on amendments in the full House of Representatives, which would probably have involved Antifederalists putting forward structural amendments, might have been offensive to many Federalists and might have posed a grave threat to the entire project of amendments in the first House of Representatives. The procedure of confining the initial discussion of amendments to a select committee was probably a major source of reassurance for Federalists.

Chapter 5

The Debate of August 13, 1789

The Dynamics of the Debate of August 13, 1789

The Select Committee appointed on July 21, 1789 to consider amendments worked in an expeditious fashion. It was as early as August 13, 1789 that Richard Bland Lee moved that the House should consider the report, sitting as a Committee of the Whole. The motion occasioned another procedural debate on whether or not to debate amendments and it is the purpose of this chapter to examine this debate.

Representative Lee's motion was seconded by John Page, who continued to support amendments to secure the rights and liberties of American citizens under the new Constitution. However, Theodore Sedgwick was opposed to the motion:

> Mr. SEDGWICK was sorry that the motion was made, because he looked upon this as a very improper time to enter upon the consideration of a subject which would undoubtedly consume many days; and when they had so much other and more important business requiring immediate attention, he begged gentlemen to recollect that all they had hitherto done was of little or no effect; their impost and tonnage laws were but a dead letter. (Gales (1834, 704))

James Madison responded to Sedgwick. Here is part of the record of his speech:

> He would remind gentlemen that there were many who conceived amendments of some kind necessary and proper in themselves; while others who are not so well satisfied of the necessity and propriety, may think they are rendered expedient from some other consideration. Is it desirable to keep up a division among the people of the United States on a point in which they consider their most essential rights are concerned? If this is an object worthy the attention of such a numerous part of our constituents, why should we decline taking it into consideration, and thereby promote that spirit of urbanity and unanimity which the Government itself stands in need of for its more full support?
>
> Already has the subject been delayed much longer than could have been

wished. If after having fixed a day for taking it into consideration, we should put it off again, a spirit of jealousy may be excited, and not allayed without great inconvenience. (Gales (1834, 704))

Stylistically, it is worth noting that like his opponents in the debate of June 8, 1789, Madison employed rhetorical questions here. Their emphasis is on securing agreement on the propositional content of the expected answer. Thus the expected answer to the first rhetorical question is along the lines 'surely it is not desirable to keep up a division on a point in which the people of the United States consider their most essential rights are concerned'. The key proposition on which Madison seeks agreement here is in the subordinate clause and thus presented by the form of the sentence as being something presupposed, namely that a bill of rights is needed to secure the most essential rights of the people.

Madison's argument, as reported, thus centered on an appeal to a spirit of generosity and urbanity on the part of Federalists, which had likewise been a theme of his major address in June.

John Vining, who had been opposed to the early consideration of amendments in June 1789, was now in favor:

Mr. VINING, impressed by the anxiety which the honorable gentleman from Virginia had discovered for having the subject of amendments considered, had agreed in his own mind, to waive, for the present, the call he was well authorized to make, for the House to take into consideration the bill of establishing a Land Office for the disposal of the vacant lands in the Western Territory. (Gales (1834, 704))

As in the previous chapter, it is worth noting how respectful Vining was towards Madison, as shown by the address form used. Vining was willing to yield to Madison.

Theodore Sedgwick spoke next:

Mr. SEDGWICK hoped the House would not consume their time in a lengthy discussion upon what business should be done first. He was of opinion that there were several matters before them of more importance than the present; and he believed the people abroad were neither anxious nor jealous about it: but if they were, they would be satisfied at the delay, when they were informed of the cause. He begged, therefore, that the question proposed by the gentleman from Virginia (Mr. LEE) might be put without further debate. (Gales (1834, 704))

Sedgwick thus expressed disagreement with Madison's assessment of how the people viewed the project of amendments, asserting that the people were not anxious about amendments. Presumably, it is a fair inference that Sedgwick continued to be opposed to the early consideration of amendments.

William Smith spoke next, in opposition to Lee's motion:

> An honorable gentleman from Virginia observed to us that these propositions
> were self-evident, that little or no debate can grow out of them. That may be his
> opinion, but truly, sir, it is not mine; for I think some of them are not self-evident, and
> some of them will admit of lengthy discussion; and some others, I hope, may be
> rejected, while their place may be better supplied by others hereafter to be brought
> forward. (Gales (1834, 705))

After Thomas Hartley had also voiced opposition to Lee's motion, Elbridge
Gerry similarly opposed it, arguing that the subject of amendments would occasion
"more copious debate" than Madison contemplated. He was also concerned that
there might be an attempt to limit discussion to the amendments in the report of the
committee.

John Lawrence, speaking next, also opposed Lee's motion:

> Mr. LAWRENCE had no objection to consider amendments at a proper time, but
> did not think that the present was a proper time to enter upon them, nor did he
> suppose that gentlemen would be precluded from a full discussion of the whole
> subject whenever it was taken up. Gentlemen would find him ready to acquiesce in
> every thing that was proper, but he could not consent to let the great business of
> legislation stand still, and thereby incur an absolute evil in order to rid themselves of
> an imaginary one; for whether the subject of amendments was considered now or at a
> more distant period, appeared to his mind a matter of mere indifference. It may further
> be observed, that few, if any, of the State Assemblies are now in session;
> consequently, the business could not be completed even if Congress had already done
> their part; but certainly the people in general are more anxious to see the Government
> in operation, than speculative amendments upon an untried Constitution. (Gales
> (1834, 706))

Lawrence's remarks reflect a continuing Federalist distaste for the business of
amendments: he viewed the evil that amendments were supposed to address as an
"imaginary one" and the amendments themselves, in his view, continued to be
"speculative." It is recalled that on June 8, 1789 he did not reject the subject of
amendments, and there were protestations in his speech now that he would have no
objection to considering amendments "at the proper time." Even so, there must be
some suspicion that he might have been indulging in the fallacy of *ad socordiam*
when asking for a postponement.

At this point James Madison rose for the second time in the debate:

> Mr. MADISON.—I beg leave to make one or two remarks more, in consequence
> of the observations which have fallen from the different sides of the House. Some

gentlemen seem to think that additional propositions will be brought forward; whether they will or not I cannot pretend to say; but if they are, I presume they will be no impediment to our deciding upon those contained in the report. But gentlemen who introduce these propositions will see that, if they are to produce more copious debate than has hitherto taken place, they will consume a great part of the remainder of the session. I wish the subject well considered, but I do not wish to see any unnecessary waste of time; and gentlemen will please to remember that this subject has yet to go before the Senate.

I admit, with the worthy gentleman who preceded me, that a great number of the community are solicitous to see the Government carried into operation; but I believe that there is a considerable part also anxious to secure those rights which they are apprehensive are endangered by the present Constitution. Now, considering the full confidence they reposed at the time of its adoption in their future representatives, I think we ought to pursue the subject to effect. I confess it has already appeared to me, in point of candor and good faith, as well as policy, to be incumbent on the first Legislature of the United States, at their first session, to make such alterations in the Constitution as will give satisfaction, without injuring or destroying any of its vital principles.

I should not press the subject at this time, because I am well aware of the importance of the other business enumerated by the gentlemen who are adverse to the present motion, but from an apprehension that, if it is delayed until the other is gone through, gentlemen's patience and application will be so harassed and fatigued as to oblige them to leave it in an unfinished state until the next session; ... (Gales (1834, 706 f.))

This speech by Madison, produced almost in its entirety here, was his last effort before what turned out to be the final procedural vote. In the speech he showed his understanding of the realities of the situation and his awareness that time was running out for the project. At the same time, he again sought to reassure his Federalist colleagues, on whose position the business depended, that he would not want to see any waste of time in the consideration of amendments. Further, he reassured them that the amendments that he had in mind would not endanger the "vital principles" of the Constitution, again emphasizing that he would not countenance structural amendments.

Speaking after Madison, William Smith remained unconvinced by Madison's argument, while Thomas Fitzsimons urged that a vote should be taken, without revealing his own sentiments on the motion. After Fitzsimons, John Page made a final appeal for Lee's motion. Here is part of this final speech:

He begged gentleman to consider the importance of the number of citizens who were anxious for amendments; if these had been added to those who openly opposed the Constitution, it possibly might have met a different fate. Can the

Government, under these circumstances, possess energy, as some gentlemen suppose? Is not the confidence of the people absolutely necessary to support it? (Gales (1834, 707))

The first of these final rhetorical questions has an emphasis on the propositional content. Page is seeking to get his audience to accept the content of the expected answer, which is along the lines 'surely, the government cannot under these circumstances, that is, without a Bill of Rights, possess energy'. The assertion contained in the final question is similarly that a Bill of Rights is needed to secure the confidence of the people for the Government. Since Federalists were anxious to establish an energetic Federal government, Page, it may be inferred, had them in mind when making his appeal.

After Page's speech, the House finally voted: "The question was now put, and carried in the affirmative" (Gales (1834, 707)).

After the vote, the House started with the immediate consideration of the substance of amendments and of the report of the select committee.

Assessing the Debate of August 13, 1789

From the point of view of assessing the significance of the procedural debate of August 13, 1789, it would have been of great historical interest to have further information on the vote at the end of the debate, for instance, on how close it was and who voted on which side. It will probably be impossible now ever to recover this information. To judge by the debate, there may have been quite a number of Federalists who voted against Lee's motion. The analyst is particularly struck by the rather dismissive and even derogatory tone that John Lawrence used in his remarks in the debate. Further, Theodore Sedgwick, to judge by the tone of his remarks, probably also voted against the motion.

While it is idle to speculate extensively on what would have happened if the vote had gone the other way and whether, in this case, the project of amendments could ever have been resurrected, it must be stated that the fate of the Bill of Rights would not have been assured if this had happened. It is clear from the remarks of several Federalists that many of them continued to view the project with suspicion and with skepticism, or at least as something of little or no importance. And time was not on the side of the project of a Bill of Rights, since only a few years later there began to be sentiment in favor of censuring Democratic societies and enacting a Sedition Act. In the changed atmosphere there would have been no hope for a Bill of Rights in anything like its present form.

At the same time, it is clear from the debate that there were Federalists who voted for Lee's motion. John Vining is the best example. This Federalist had a great deal of respect for James Madison, as is clear from the record: he was "impressed by the anxiety which the honorable gentleman from Virginia had discovered for having the subject of amendments considered" (Gales (1834, 740)).

Vining's comment once again emphasizes Madison's central role in the project of amendments. Indeed, to judge by the evidence of the debates of June 8, July 21 and August 13, 1789, it is clear that without Madison's personal stature and without his perseverance, the project would never have got anywhere in the first House of Representatives. Even if it had somehow got as far as the debate of August 13, 1789, it might well have been terminated on that day if Madison had not been there to argue for it.

What also deserves to be emphasized is the content of Madison's argumentation and his sensitivity to his audience. This was the third procedural debate concerned with the question of whether or not to debate amendments in a timely fashion, and certain Federalists were again objecting to the project. Under the circumstances Madison could have been forgiven for feeling tired of the tactics of obstruction. However, he did not lose his composure. Instead, he patiently reassured Federalists again and again that no time would be wasted and that no structural amendments would be approved. By addressing the concerns of Federalists in this way, Madison was able to prevail in the end, with the House of Representatives at last voting to end the series of procedural debates on whether or not to debate the project of amendments in a timely fashion and deciding to do so without further delay.

As a coda to this chapter, it may be added that after the vote the House of Representatives proceeded immediately to consider amendments. Within a few days the set of amendments were ready for consideration by the Senate. By the end of September 1789 the two Houses had agreed on the precise wording of the amendments to be submitted to the States for ratification and by the end of 1791 the requisite number of States had ratified those amendments that constitute the Bill of Rights.

Chapter 6

James Madison on Freedom of Speech in 1794

Introduction

In 1794 there was an insurrection, the so-called Whiskey Rebellion, against the excise tax on spirits and the power of the Federal Government in the four Western counties of Pennsylvania. In a speech to the two Houses of Congress on November 19, 1794, President Washington included the following passage:

> In the four western counties of Pennsylvania, a prejudice, fostered and embittered by the artifice of men, who labored for an ascendancy over the will of others, by the guidance of their passions, produced symptoms of riot and violence. It is well known, that Congress did not hesitate to examine the complaints which were presented; and to relieve them, as far as justice dictated, or general convenience would permit. But, the impression which this moderation made on the discontented, did not correspond with what it deserved. The arts of delusion were no longer confined to the efforts of designing individuals. The very forbearance to press prosecutions was misinterpreted into a fear of urging the execution of the laws; and associations of men began to denounce threats against the officers employed. From a belief, that, by a more formal concert, their operation might be defeated, certain self-created societies assumed the tone of condemnation. Hence, while the greater part of Pennsylvania itself were conforming themselves to the acts of excise, a few counties were resolved to frustrate them. (*Debates* (1849, 787 f.))

The part significant for present purposes was Washington's reprobating reference to "certain self-created societies." This designation was widely taken to refer to Democratic societies. These were societies that were devoted to promoting Republican ideas and ideals in the new Republic. They were active for instance in Pennsylvania, but much less so in New England States, which tended to be more Federalist in outlook.

The Senate quickly decided to express its support for Washington's criticism of Democratic societies. Only two days later it adopted a report that included the following statement:

Our anxiety, arising from the licentious and open resistance to the laws in the Western counties of Pennsylvania, has been increased by the proceedings of certain self-created societies, relative to the laws and administration of the Government; proceedings, in our apprehension, founded in political error, calculated, if not intended, to disorganize our Government, and which, by inspiring delusive hopes of support, have been influential in misleading our fellow-citizens in the scene of insurrection: (*Debates* (1849, 794))

A similar statement was offered to the House of Representatives by Thomas Fitzsimons on November 24, 1794:

"As part of this subject, we cannot withhold our reprobation of the self-created societies, which have risen up in some parts of the Union, misrepresenting the conduct of the Government, and disturbing the operation of the laws, and which, by deceiving and inflaming the ignorant and the weak, may naturally be supposed to have stimulated and urged the insurrection." (*Debates* (1849, 899))

The proposed amendment led to a prolonged debate in the House of Representatives. The debate is of significance because it sheds light on how the concept of freedom of expression was understood at this early period in American history. When discussing this question, it is also advisable to take account of the political split between Federalists and emerging Jeffersonian Republicans and to relate views on freedom of expression to this split. James Madison, who had been a prominent Federalist in 1789, was now a leading Republican.

A full speech-by-speech account of the prolonged debate cannot be given here. However, it is worth sampling some of the highlights and some of the main types of arguments that were put forward.

The Debate of November 24, 1794

Representative Giles was the first speaker to object to the amendment. He linked the proposed amendment censuring Democratic societies to freedom of expression. Here is part of the record:

Gentlemen were interfering with a delicate right, and they would be much wiser to let the Democratic societies alone. ... Members are not sent here to deal out applauses or censures in this way. Mr. G. rejected all aiming at a restraint on the opinions of private persons. (*Debates* (1849, 900 f.))

By contrast, Representative W. Smith, speaking in support of the motion against

Democratic societies soon afterwards, said that "the whole of their proceedings has been a chain of censures on the conduct of Government," and "complained in strong terms, of the calumnies and slanders which they had propagated against Government" (*Debates* (1849, 901 f.))

Representative Tracy also argued in favor of the amendment:

> The Democratic societies form but a very small portion of the people of America. Where is the harm in saying that one hundredth, or, I believe I might say, not more than one thousandth part of the citizens of the United States have been mistaken, and that they have been imprudent in printing certain indiscreet resolutions? Mr. T. declared that if the President had not spoke of the matter, he should have been willing to let it alone, because whenever a subject of that kind was touched, there were certain gentlemen in that House who shook their backs, like a sore-backed horse, and cried out The Liberties of the people! Mr. T. wished only that the House, if their opinion of these societies corresponded with that of the PRESIDENT, should declare that they had such an opinion. This was quite different from attempting to legislate on the subject. Had not the Legislature done so before? Is there any impropriety in paying this mark of respect to a man to whom all America owes such indelible obligations? He thought that this declaration from the House of Representatives would tend to discourage Democratic societies, by uniting all men of sense against them. (*Debates* (1849, 903))

The appeal to the authority of the President found here was a common theme in Federalist speeches. It brings to mind the fallacy of *ad verecundiam,* or appeal to authority. This fallacy "means appeal to reverence (respect) and refers to the fallacy of inappropriate use of appeals to expert opinion in argumentation" (Walton (1995, 46)). The House of Representatives was forming an opinion on whether to censure Democratic societies, and to the extent that an appeal to authority may have hindered the discussion of the merits of the issue at hand, relating to the role of Democratic societies, it is possible to speak of a fallacy. Tracy declared that he would have left Democratic societies alone if the President had not spoken, but many Federalists took up the theme of censuring these societies with such gusto that the observer may wonder whether there may not have been an element of pretension in such declarations.

Representative Nicholas opposed the proposed vote of censure. His reason is worth noting:

> ... It was wrong to condemn societies for particular acts. That there never should be a Democratical society in America, said Mr. N., I would give my most hearty consent; but I cannot agree to persecution for the sake of opinions. With respect either to the propriety or the power of suppressing them, Mr. N. was in both cases equally of opinion that it was much better to let them alone. They must stand or fall by the general sentiments of the people of America. (*Debates* (1849, 905))

The key statement here is "I cannot agree to persecution for the sake of opinions." This articulated the intellectual position of those opposed to censuring Democratic societies in a succinct way.

The Debate of November 25, 1794

The House of Representatives continued the debate on Tuesday, November 25, 1794. The first speaker was Representative Murray, and he laid out the intellectual position of Federalists pushing for the censure motion in a way that serves as a counterpoint to the intellectual position articulated by Representative Nicholas on the previous day. Here is part of the record of what he said:

> This amendment to the *Address* would operate as advice. It curtails not the right of a free press, which Mr. M. held to be the luminary of the public mind. It would tend to excite a judicious and salutary inquiry among many respecting the just and true limits within which a virtuous and enlightened well-wisher to our country would think it safe to exercise this right. (*Debates* (1849, 906))

While protesting that the amendment would not abridge the right of a free press, Murray was in fact advocating limitations within which it would be "safe to exercise this right." The free expression of opinions, advocated by Nicholas, was thus unacceptable to this Federalist.

The sentiment of Representative Nicholas was echoed by Representative Venable, who said in part: "The people have a right to think and a right to speak. I am not afraid to speak my sentiments" (*Debates* (1849, 910)).

By contrast, Theodore Sedgwick strongly favored the amendment. Speaking of Democratic societies, he said in part:

> They should have told what was well done as well as ill done. From Portland, in Maine, to the other end of the Continent, have they ever approved of one single act? They have scrutinized with eagle eyes into every fault. Whom are we to trust, them, or the man that, more than any other human man ever did, possesses the affection of a whole people? The question is, shall we support the Constitution or not? (*Debates* (1849, 912))

Sedgwick did not thus shy away from prescribing to Democratic societies what they should report on. He proceeded to an appeal to authority, capping the appeal by claiming that failure to pass the amendment would be tantamount to failing to support the Constitution. Sedgwick's remarks serve to show the depth of Federalist feeling in favor of limiting the expression of opinions.

At the end of the debate on that day, a vote was taken and the words "self-created societies" were struck out of the amendment, by a vote of 47 to 45.

The Debate of November 26, 1794

In spite of the vote on November 25, 1794, the intense debate on whether to censure self-created societies continued on the following day, Wednesday, November 26, 1794. Initiating the discussion, Representative Dayton moved to reinstate the words struck out the previous day. Representative Rutherford spoke against the motion, saying in part:

> Perhaps Democratic societies have sometimes done wrong, but this was not a proper foundation for condemning them in whole. Every Government under Heaven hath a tendency to degenerate into tyranny. Let the people then speak out. *Why not let them speak out?* (*Debates* (1849, 915, the emphasis in the original)

Representative Giles similarly argued against censuring Democratic societies. At one point he picked up a Federalist theme that it was appropriate for the House to censure the public. Here is part of the record of what he said:

> It had been said, that when people censured the House, that the House were entitled to return the compliment by censuring them. This position Mr. G. denied. No, sir, said he, the public have a right to censure us, and we have *not* a right to censure them. We have a title, as individuals, but when we undertake this business in the shape of a Legislative body, we are as much a self-created society, as any Democratic club in the Union. We are neither authorized by the Constitution, nor paid by the citizens of the United States, for assuming the office of censorship. ... Many people ... condemn the proceedings of the Democratic societies, yet will not choose to see them divested of the inalienable privilege of thinking, of speaking, of writing, and of printing. (*Debates* (1849, 917 f.), the emphasis in the original)

At the end of the proceedings for the day, Fisher Ames delivered a very long speech. At one point he said:

> Is it possible for any to be so deluded as to suppose that the over-zeal for Government, on the part of the supporters of this amendment, would prompt them to desire or to attempt the obstruction of the liberty of speech, or the genuine freedom of the press? (*Debates* (1849, 924))

What is significant here is the modifier "genuine" that Fisher Ames inserted in front of "freedom of the press."

The Debates of November 27 and 28, 1794

The intense debate on the question of whether to censure Democratic societies
continued on November 27. It was on this day that James Madison joined in for the
first time. Here is part of the record of what the Father of the First Amendment had
to say:

> He conceived it to be a sound principle, that an action innocent in the eye of the law
> could not be the object of censure to a Legislative body. When the people have
> formed a Constitution, they retain those rights which they have not expressly
> delegated. It is a question whether what is retained can be legislated upon. Opinions
> are not the objects of legislation. You animadvert on the abuse of reserved rights: how
> far will this go? It may extend to the liberty of speech, and of the press. It is in vain to
> say that this indiscriminate censure is no punishment. If it falls on classes, or
> individuals, it will be a severe punishment. ... If we advert to the nature of Republican
> Government, we shall find that the censorial power is in the people over the
> Government, and not in the Government over the people. As he had confidence in the
> good sense and patriotism of the people, he did not anticipate any lasting evil to result
> from the publications of these societies; they will stand or fall by the public opinion;
> no line can be drawn in this case. (*Debates* (1849, 934 f.))

Madison thus found a succinct way to reject the Federalist attempt to censure
Republican societies: "opinions are not the objects of legislation."

Representative Dexter, speaking next, presented a Federalist response to
Madison. He said in part:

> Can I be a freeman, sir, if the Government, which is my only security for all my rights,
> may be invaded with impunity, and my reputation, the dearest of all possessions and
> the best reward of virtue, blasted by the foul breath of slander and falsehood? When
> this shall be admitted as a principle in the American code, we shall call that freedom
> which will be our misery; we shall cease to deserve liberty; we shall need a master.
> Let men meet for deliberating on public matters; let them freely express their opinions
> in conversation or in print, but let them do this with a decent respect for the will of the
> majority, and for the Government and rulers which the people have appointed; let
> them not become a band of conspirators, to make and propagate falsehood and
> slander; ... (*Debates* (1849, 936))

Dexter's theme is thus similar to that of earlier Federalist speakers: while
professing respect for free discussion, he emphasized that the discussion of public
matters should be guided or limited by a sense of respect for the government and

the rulers, with the government being the only guarantor of rights.

Dexter went on, according to the record:

> Mr. D. observed, that Mr. MADISON had stated as a principle from which to argue, and on which almost all his deductions were founded, a proposition so doubtful in itself, that it ought rather to be proved, than assumed as a first principle from which to reason, viz. that we cannot rightfully intermeddle in any way with a subject which we cannot regulate by law. Admitting it to be a true and self-evident proposition, however, he said, it concluded nothing against the amendment: for it would still remain to be proved, which it never could be, that the Legislature had no right to restrain such abuses by law. (*Debates* (1849, 937))

Dexter thus argued that Congress could enact a law to restrict freedom of expression so that it might fulfill what he took to be the required standard of respect for the government. He was thus ready to go further than some of his Federalist colleagues in 1794.

For his part, Representative Nicholas continued to insist on the proposition that falsehoods will be defeated by public opinion and on the right of Democratic societies to criticize the Government:

> Noticing Mr. Dexter's remarks on the abuse of the liberty of the press, he adverted to the publications of the Democratic societies; if they are so false as is pretended, they will defeat themselves. He noticed the concession which had been made, that societies for political information are legal, and may be useful: taking this for granted, he insisted that they had a right to censure as well as to inform; for, without this right, the concession amounts to nothing. (*Debates* (1849, 940))

Representative Carnes also rose to support the Republican standpoint. Here is part of the record:

> A gentleman [Mr. SEDGWICK] told you the other day, that Democratic societies had produced the insurrection; but when, in the course of his observations, he became a little more animated, he told us that a foreign Envoy, *Genet,* had been the cause of all this mischief. If this be true, the Democratic societies are innocent. Sir, by this amendment you would prevent the freedom of speech, and lock the mouths of men. They are not to censure the measures of Government, and then bad men may do what they please with it. I hope, sir, that the day will never come, when the people of America shall not have leave to assemble, and speak their mind. (*Debates* (1849, 941))

After one or two other speeches, the House of Representatives finally took a series of votes. The insertion of the words "self-created societies" in the resolution was first approved by a vote of 47 to 45, but then an additional change, limiting the application of the motion to censuring "certain self-created societies and combinations of men" to "the four Western counties of Pennsylvania and parts adjacent," was also carried, with the casting vote of the Speaker, after a tie of 46 to 46. Afterwards the whole amendment was rejected.

The House of Representatives came back to the task of formulating a response to President Washington the following day. On this day, members, after little discussion, at last approved a formulation that omitted the controversial phrase "certain self-created societies." The salient sentence was approved in the following form:

> And we learn, with the greatest concern, that any misrepresentations whatever, of the Government and its proceedings, either by individuals or combinations of men, should have been made, and so far credited as to foment the flagrant outrage which has been committed on the laws. (*Debates* (1849, 947))

With this, the discussion of the President's speech, including its theme relating to freedom of speech, came to an end.

Assessing the Debates of November 1794

The debate of 1794 ended with an ostensible victory for the Madisonian side, in the sense that the words "certain self-created societies" were omitted from the response of the House of Representatives.

The debates also had a much broader significance. They defined two broad positions on what freedom of expression and of the press meant and should mean in the new Republic.

It is also possible to associate the two positions with the two political parties, Federalists and Republicans. The Federalist position in 1794 was to pay homage to the principle of freedom of expression, but to emphasize at the same time that there should be limits on political discussion and on the criticism of the government and of rulers. Once such limits were placed on political discussion, genuine liberty was achieved. The introduction of the modifier *genuine,* as noted in Fisher Ames's speech above, is significant, in that it signified a more restrictive interpretation of the concept.

Some Federalists were even ready to pass legislation to secure limits on freedom of speech, to achieve what they regarded as genuine freedom of speech. The precise nature of the legislation did not come up in the discussion in 1794, for obvious reasons, but their readiness to pass such legislation is worth noting.

For their part, Republicans had a broader notion of freedom of speech. They were reluctant to limit political discussion by means of legislation, or even by means of a vote of censure directed at Democratic societies. Instead they looked to the people and to public opinion to winnow out falsehoods and slanders. Republicans thus did not want to exempt the government and the rulers of the state from criticism. Madison was the one to express the Republican position most succinctly when he observed that "opinions are not the objects of legislation" (*Debates* (1849, 934)).

Chapter 7

The Federalist Triumph: the Sedition Act of 1798

Introduction

It was seen in the previous chapter how two contrasting approaches to the concept of freedom of speech had emerged in the new Republic by 1794. On the one hand, Republicans had a broad notion of freedom of speech, permitting the free expression of opinions, unhindered by Federal legislation. On the other, Federalists wanted to secure what was termed "genuine" freedom of speech, which was to be achieved by the imposition of limits on freedom of discussion, particularly on the extent to which the government and rulers could be criticized with impunity.

The precise nature of the limits on freedom of speech that Federalists had in mind did not emerge in the debates in November 1794, and the attempt to censure Democratic societies was eventually voted down in the House of Representatives. However, less than four years later, Federalists were back with a vengeance.

In the summer of 1798 the Federalist majority in Congress approved four acts that subsequently came to be known as the Alien and Sedition Acts. When discussing these acts, historians sympathetic to Federalists tend to concentrate on the Alien Acts, as if these had more significance than the Sedition Act. However, the Alien Acts had little practical or conceptual impact. By contrast, it is the Sedition Act that merits attention, because of its content and the philosophical and conceptual underpinning of that content. In brief, the Sedition Act constituted the most serious actual and conceptual threat to freedom of speech that has materialized to this day. It is therefore important to any investigation dealing with the emergence of the American conception of freedom of speech.

The Sedition Act was pushed through by Federalists against fierce Republican opposition in the House of Representatives in early July 1798. It was signed into law by President Adams on July 14, 1798.

The purpose of this chapter is to examine the rhetoric that Federalists used to justify the Act and the rhetoric that was used by Republicans to oppose it.

It is easy to understand the threat that the Act posed to freedom of expression when one reads it. Here is the text of the Sedition Act, or of the Act for the Punishment of Certain Crimes:

An Act, in addition to the act, entitled, "An act for the punishment of certain crimes against the United States."

Be it enacted, &c., That if any persons shall unlawfully combine or conspire together, with intent to oppose any measure or measures of the Government of the United States, which are or shall be directed by proper authority, or to impede the operation of any law of the United States, or to intimidate or prevent any person holding a place or office in or under the Government of the United States, from undertaking, performing, or executing, his trust or duty; and if any person or persons, with intent as aforesaid, shall counsel, advise, or attempt to procure, any insurrection, riot, unlawful assembly or combination, whether such conspiracy, threatening, counsel, advice, or attempt, shall have the proposed effect or not, he or they shall be deemed guilty of a high misdemeanor, and on conviction, before any court of the United States having jurisdiction thereof, shall be punished by a fine not exceeding five thousand dollars, and by imprisonment during a term not less than six months, nor exceeding five years; and, further, at the discretion of the court, may be holden to find sureties for his good behaviour in such sum, and for such time, as the said court may direct.

SEC. 2. *And be it further enacted,* That if any person shall write, print, utter, or publish, or shall cause or procure to be written, printed, uttered, or published, or shall knowingly and willingly assist or aid in writing, printing, uttering, or publishing, any false, scandalous, and malicious, writing or writings against the Government of the United States, or either House of the Congress of the United States, or the President of the United States, with intent to defame the said Government, or either House of the said Congress, or the said President, or to bring them, or either of them, into contempt or disrepute; or to excite against them, or either or any of them, the hatred of the good people of the United States, or to stir up sedition within the United States; or to excite any unlawful combinations therein, for opposing or resisting any law of the United States, or any act of the President of the United States, done in pursuance of any such law, or of the powers in him vested by the Constitution of the United States, or to resist, oppose, or defeat any such law or act; or to aid, encourage, or abet, any hostile designs of any foreign nation against the United States, their people or Government, then such persons, being thereof convicted, before any court of the United States having jurisdiction thereof, shall be punished by a fine not exceeding two thousand dollars, and by imprisonment not exceeding two years.

SEC. 3. *And be it further enacted,* That if any person shall be prosecuted, under this act, for the writing or publishing any libel, aforesaid, it shall be lawful for the defendant, upon the trial of the cause, to give in evidence, in his defence, the truth of the matter contained in the publication charged as a libel. And the jury, who shall try the cause, shall have a right to determine the law and the fact, under the direction of the court, as in other cases.

SEC. 4. *And be it further enacted,* That this act shall continue and be in force until the third day of March, one thousand eight hundred and one, and no longer: *Provided,* That the expiration of the act shall not prevent or defeat a prosecution and punishment of any offence against the law, during the time it shall be in force.

Approved, July 14, 1798. (*Debates* (1851a, 3776 f.))

It was seen in chapters 3, 4, and 5 how the Federalist majority had needed to be coaxed and cajoled into approving the Bill of Rights in the summer of 1789, when three grueling procedural debates were required before the majority were willing to consider the issue. No such procedural procrastination occurred in the case of the Sedition Act. Instead the Federalist majority was eager to act quickly and they rushed the Act through the House of Representatives in about a week in early July 1798.

Here is an encyclopedic summary of the factors that created conditions favorable to the adoption of the Alien and Sedition Acts:

Ostensibly intended to safeguard the country during time of war, these acts also originated in the Federalists' alarm at the growing strength of the Republican party led by Thomas Jefferson and James Madison; the intemperate and slanderous attacks made upon administration leaders by Republican journalists; and the widespread fear of the "foreign menace" represented by French agents and refugee Irish and English radicals. (Miller (1997, 579))

An additional factor was the unclear status of a presumed common law of libel at that time. There was a Federalist inspired attempt to invoke such a law against Benjamin Bache, a leading Republican newspaper man, just prior to the adoption of the Sedition Act. Here is an account of this attempt:

On June 27, 1798, two weeks before the sedition bill was signed by the President, Bache was arrested on a warrant issued by Justice Richard Peters of the United States Supreme Court, charging him with having libeled the President and the government in a manner tending to excite sedition and opposition to the laws.

This indictment was made at common law without benefit of statutory authority. According to the commonly accepted Federalist theory, this was entirely legal because the government of the United States enjoyed jurisdiction over all crimes and misdemeanors punishable at common law. ...

And yet Bache had no serious apprehension that the government's case would stand in court. Justice Samuel Chase of the United States Supreme Court had a few months before declared his opinion that, in the absence of express statute, the Federal government could not support such prosecutions. ...

The Federalists, too, were aware that in view of Justice Chase's opinion, Bache and other "Jacobins" might escape punishment if the Federal government trusted to its presumed authority under the common law. This prospect spurred efforts to secure the speedy passage of the Sedition Act. Since the powers of the Federal government to act in cases of libel and sedition were questioned, its authority must be affirmed by the enactment of a law expressly giving it such powers. [note omitted, JR] (Miller (1951, 65 f.))

Federalists also had a British model: the British Sedition Act had been enacted some four years earlier, with Britain at war with France. That act "provided for punishment of anyone writing, publishing, or speaking so as to bring his majesty or the government in contempt or to arouse hatred against them" (Dauer (1953, 158)). It thus "became possible to speak and write as well as to act treason" (Miller (1951, 68)).

Federalists, drawing inspiration from the British law, thus saw an opportunity to achieve their aims:

> It was this system [the British system, JR] that the Federalists proposed to copy, although the United States was still technically at peace with France. But in giving their votes to the sedition bill, many Federalists had other objectives in mind than their ostensible purpose of protecting the country from the machinations of French agents: like the Naturalization Act, it was intended to injure the Republican party by striking at freedom of the press. (Miller (1951, 69))

There were two major debates in the House of Representatives on the Sedition Act in early July 1798, the first one on July 5 and the second one on July 10. In the debates Republicans tried to slow down Federalists and to engage them in argumentation about the proposed Act. These debates are examined in this chapter, with the focus on the arguments used by the two sides. The data come from *The Debates and Proceedings in the Congress of the United States,* abbreviated as *Debates* (1851a).

Republicans failed in their attempt to stop Federalists in their rush to enact the Sedition Act. However, the argumentation used brought conceptions of what freedom of speech was taken to mean in the early Republic into a sharp focus, and the debates are of great significance when tracing the forging of freedom of expression in American history.

The Debate of July 5, 1798

The debate of July 5, 1798 was initiated by Harrison Otis, a prominent Federalist, who moved that the Act for the punishment of certain crimes against the United States — the Sedition Act — be read a second time.[1] Representative Harrison, a Republican, thereupon "called for the reading of the amendments to the

Constitution" (*Debates* (1851a, 2093)). This precipitated a statement from the Speaker ruling that "the only motion in order, if objections were made to the second reading of this bill, would be to reject this bill," whereupon "Mr. LIVINGSTON made that motion" (*Debates* (1851a, 2093)).

The next speaker was John Allen, one of the most influential and active Federalists of the time. (On Allen's role in the later debate aimed at barring Representative Matthew Lyon, a Republican member from Vermont, from the House of Representatives after he had served his sentence imposed under the Sedition Act, see Rudanko (2001, 89 f.).) Early on in his speech, he referred to a paragraph in the *Aurora,* a Republication newspaper, on negotiations with France:

Mr. ALLEN.— I hope this bill will not be rejected. If ever there was a nation which required a law of this kind, it is this. Let gentleman look at certain papers printed in this city and elsewhere, and ask themselves whether an unwarrantable and dangerous combination does not exist to overturn and ruin the Government by publishing the most shameless falsehoods against the Representatives of the people of all denominations, that they are hostile to free Governments and genuine liberty, and of course to the welfare of this country; that they ought, therefore, to be displaced, and that the people ought to raise an *insurrection* against the Government.

In the *Aurora,* of the 28th of June last, we see this paragraph: "It is a curious fact, America is making war with France for *not* treating at the very moment the Minister for Foreign Affairs fixes upon the very day for opening a negotiation with Mr. Gerry. What think you of this, Americans!"

Such paragraphs need but little comment. The public agents are charged with crimes, for which, if true, they ought to be hung. The intention here is to persuade the people that peace with France is in our power; nay, that she is sincerely desirous of it, on proper terms, but that we reject her offers, and proceed to plunge our country into a destructive war.

This combination against our peace is extensive; it embraces characters whose stations demand a different course. Is this House free from it? Recollect what a few days ago fell from the very gentleman (Mr. LIVINGSTON,) who now so boldly and violently calls on us to reject this bill at the instant of its coming before us, without suffering it to be read a second time. The gentleman proposed a resolution requesting the President to instruct Mr. Gerry to conclude a treaty with the French Government; and declared that "he believed a negotiation might be opened, and that it was probable a treaty might be concluded which it would be honorable to the United States to accept. He did not wish to frustrate so happy an event by any punctilio, because they had refused to treat with three Envoys, but were willing to treat with one." This is in the very spirit of the malicious paragraph I just now read. It is pursuing the same systematic course of operations. The gentleman also said (what has not been published, however,) that "the commission of the Envoys being joint and several, Mr. Gerry had unquestionably ample powers to treat alone." Here are circumstances of what I call *a combination against the Government,* in attempts to persuade the people of certain facts, which a majority of this House, at least, and of the people at large, I believe, know to be unfounded. Who can say that Mr. Gerry has the power to treat alone, or that the French Government is willing to treat with him on fair and honorable terms? Gentlemen do not believe either, let them say what they will. Does such a commission empower one to exercise the functions of the whole in opposition to the opinions of his colleagues? It would produce the most inextricable confusion. The severalty of the powers is well known always to be a provision against such accidents as may prevent or disable a part of the Commissioners from acting. I mention these things to show what false ideas gentlemen endeavor to impress the public mind with on this subject. (*Debates* (1851a, 2093 f.))

An outstanding feature of Allen's argument here is the prominence of individually named targets in it. He directs his attack against one publication, the *Aurora,* and one individual member of the House of Representatives, Representative Livingston. In the case of the attack on the Congressman, it is possible to speak of the fallacy of *ad hominem,* or argument against the person. This argument "is traditionally meant to denote the kind of argumentation that argues against somebody's argument by attacking the person who put forward the argument" (Walton (1995, 36)). Allen is saying that because Livingston had expressed what he regarded as malicious opinions on the issue of negotiating with France, he is not a person to be listened to when he "so boldly and violently" now proposes that the Act be rejected. By focusing attention on the character of the person who had moved that the bill be rejected, Allen thus sought to divert the discussion away from the merits and demerits of the Act being considered.

The attack on the newspaper is not a fallacy since it was produced as an illustration of the kind of writings that Allen wished to make punishable by law. What the newspaper had published was, in Allen's view, an exampled of "the most shameless falsehoods against the Representatives of the people."

It is worth noting here what the nature of "the most shameless falsehoods" was. The "falsehood" turned on the legal point of whether Gerry had the authority to treat alone with the French government. Whether or not he had that legal authority presumably depended on the terms on which the commission had been sent to France. That the raising of a point about the status of an individual member of the commission should have been regarded by Allen as a flagrantly shameless act that should have been punished indicated the lengths to which Federalists were prepared to go to limit freedom of speech by means of the Sedition Act.

There is another feature of Allen's speech that is worth remarking on. This is his phrase "genuine liberty." Allen was thus echoing Fisher Ames's phrase "genuine freedom of the press," used some four years earlier in a speech in a debate on Democratic societies. The addition of the modifier was symptomatic of a Federalist desire to redefine freedom of expression in a way as to place limits on it, to ensure that is "genuine."

While Allen's initial attack may not have been a convincing illustration of a shameless attack on a member of the Government, Allen proceeded to a second example:

Permit me to read a paragraph from "The Time-Piece," a paper printed in New York:

"When such a character attempts by antiquated and exploded sophistry, by Jesuitical arguments, to extinguish the sentiment of liberty, 'tis fit the mask should be torn off from this meaner species of aristocracy than history has condescended to record; where a person without patriotism, without philosophy, without a taste for the fine arts, building his pretensions on a gross and indigested compilation of statutes and precedents, is jostled into the Chief Magistracy by the ominous combination of old Tories with old opinions, and old Whigs with new, 'tis fit this mock Monarch, with his Court, composed of Tories and speculators, should pass in review before the good sense of the world. Monarchies are seen only with indignation and concern; at sight of these terrible establishments, fears accompany the execrations of mankind; but when the champion of the well-born, with his serene Court, is seen soliciting and answering Addresses, and pronouncing anathemas against France, it shall be my fault if other emotions be not excited; if to tears and execrations be not added derision and contempt."

Gentlemen contend for the liberty of opinions and of the press. Let me ask them whether they seriously think the liberty of the press authorizes such publications? The President of the United States is here called "a person without patriotism, without philosophy, and a mock monarch," and the free election of the people is pronounced "a jostling him into the Chief Magistracy by the ominous combination of old Tories, with old opinions, and old Whigs with new."

If this be not a conspiracy against Government and people, I know not what to understand from the "threat of tears, execrations, derision, and contempt." Because the Constitution guaranties the right of expressing our opinions, and the freedom of the press, am I at liberty to falsely call you a thief, a murderer, an atheist? Because I have the liberty of locomotion, of going where I please, have I a right to ride over the footman in the path? (*Debates* (1851a, 2097))

Allen's point here is at least potentially more salient than his first rather obscure legal point. The President had been called "a person without patriotism, without philosophy, and a mock monarch." This allegation ascribes several properties to the President, and the properties are of a negative or derogatory nature. One of the properties is in the nature of an epithet "a mock monarch." The intended effect of citing such properties and such epithets is to bring the intended target down, by means of using a dishonoring expression referring to the target.

However, even here it is important to note that epithets and alleged properties can be of different kinds, and that whether they are true or not can be a matter of opinion. To call a human being a dog is to use an epithet that is clearly untrue, but the characterizations cited by Allen are of an evaluative nature, and it is a matter of opinion whether and to what extent they might apply to a political figure.

In the further course of his remarks Allen put forward this argument for the Sedition Act:

> At the commencement of the Revolution in France those loud and enthusiastic advocates for liberty and equality took special care to occupy and command all the presses in the nation; they well knew the powerful influence to be obtained on the public mind by that engine; its operations are on the poor, the ignorant, the passionate, and the vicious; over all these classes of men the freedom of the press shed its baneful effects, and they all became the tools of faction and ambition, and the virtuous, the pacific, and the rich, were their victims. The Jacobins of our country, too, sir, are determined to preserve in their hands, the same weapon; it is our business to wrest it from them. Hence this motion so suddenly made, and so violently supported by the mover, to reject this bill without even suffering it to have a second reading; hence this alarm for the safety of "the freedom of speech and of the press." (*Debates* (1851a, 2098))

Allen is again engaging in a personal attack here and it is pertinent to invoke a fallacy. The fallacy here is a type of *ad hominem,* with Allen now using a broader brush than in his initial attack on Representative Livingston. He associates all those opposing the Sedition Act with French Jacobins, with Livingston no doubt intended to be prominent among them. This may be viewed as an instance of the fallacy of guilt by association. Walton describes this fallacy as follows:

> *a* is a member of or is associated with group *G,* which should be morally condemned.
> Therefore *a* is a bad person.
> Therefore *a*'s argument α should not be accepted. (Walton (1998b, 257))

Calling those opposed to the Sedition Act "the Jacobins of our country" is also to use a derogatory epithet, of the kind that Allen had just accused a critic of the Adams administration of directing at President Adams. Again the epithet is dishonoring towards its target and designed to bring the target down.

The passage is also significant because of Allen's statement that "it is our business to wrest it from them." He is saying that it is the business of Federalists to wrest the press from Republicans. The statement looks like a candid acknowledgement of a motive that Allen, a prominent Federalist, had in mind when promoting the Sedition Act. Because of its candid nature, the statement is not a fallacious argument.

One more passage deserves to be reproduced here from Allen's important speech. He quoted a member of the House of Representatives from Virginia as writing to his constituents that "the public debt has been studiously augmented and funded," and went on to make this comment:

> How could a member of this House seriously inform his constituents that "the public debt has been studiously augmented?" He knew the reverse to be true; how he could say anything else this letter contains I cannot imagine. His object must be to inflame his constituents against the Government, though at the expense of all truth. But, sir, we do know that very many of such letters have been sent into a particular quarter of the Union; and we cannot be surprised at the opinions there entertained of the Government and its administration. Gentlemen, by such measures, are planting thorns under their dying pillows. If this country is brought into a civil war, of which there is too much danger, let gentlemen lay it well to heart; I beseech them now to inquire with themselves, what they have done by such letters to contribute to that calamitous event? (*Debates* (1851a, 2101))

To the extent that Allen's argument here pertains to the type of restriction included in the Sedition Act, he is presumably saying that in the absence of the Act, newspapers may report pronouncements by members of Congress about Congress studiously augmenting the national debt, which may have such a disastrous consequence that the country is brought into a civil war. The prospect of a civil war, as a consequence of the absence of the Sedition Act, may be considered an instance of the fallacy from fear. This is a type of argument from consequences where the consequences of a particular course of action are depicted in a skewed or biased way.

Godin has noted that the argument from fear often involves exaggeration and has identified two reasons for this:

> ... first, many everyday arguments are purposely exaggerated precisely because this makes it more like they will create the incentive needed to persuade. Second, audiences readily accept exaggeration when it matches their preferences and values. (Godin (1999, 350))

In the present case the bad consequence mentioned, a civil war, no less, as resulting from a letter sent by a Congressman, at least in part, certainly suggests exaggeration. It also suggests that Allen was more concerned "to preach to the faithful," that is, to speak to Federalists, rather than attempting to persuade Republicans to vote for the Sedition Act.

Representative Harper, another influential Federalist, spoke next. Here is one point that he made:

He remembered a very respectable authority in this country (Dr. FRANKLIN) had said, in an essay of his, called "the Court of the Press," that the liberty of the press could never be suffered to exist without the liberty of the cudgel; meaning no doubt to say, that as the use of the latter must be restrained, so must also the former, or else human life would be deplorable. Nor would the rational liberty of the press be restricted by a well defined law, provided persons have a fair trial by jury; but that liberty of the press which those who desire, who wish to overturn society, and trample upon everything not their own, ought not to be allowed, either in speaking or writing, in any country. (*Debates* (1851a, 2102))

The fallacy of *ad hominem* resurfaces here, in its broadly conceived form, for Representative Harper branded those opposed to the Sedition Act as people who want "to overturn society" and to "trample upon everything not their own."

Harper's statement is prefaced with an appeal to the respected authority of Dr. Franklin. This is an example of the fallacy of *ad verecundiam*. This "means appeal to reverence (respect) and refers to the fallacy of inappropriate use of appeals to expert opinion in argumentation" (Walton (1995, 46)).

There are several different ways in which the appeal to an authority can go wrong:

We can have one type of fallacious appeal where the person cited is not really an expert and another where the person is an expert but in the wrong field. Still another type of fallacy occurs where the expert is not named or otherwise specified exactly enough. Yet another type of failure occurs where the expert is named and a genuine expert in a relevant field but her opinion is not what it is said to be. (Walton (1995, 47 f.))

In the present instance the appeal to the authority of Benjamin Franklin is weakened by the consideration that the statement was being used without regard to its proper context. Thus Harper omitted to mention that in his argument Franklin was arguing for a State law, not for a Federal law:

In the first place, Franklin's essay was directed to the legislators of Pennsylvania in an effort to get, not a national sedition law, but a state libel act. He called for a specific law to define libel so as to provide for the security of a citizen's personal reputation. Harper not only shifted Franklin's argument so as to apply to the jurisdiction of the federal government rather than to that of the states, but he expanded Franklin's recommendations to apply not only to personal reputations but to official reputations as well. (Smith (1956, 138), discussing a later reference to Franklin by Harper)

Even if the appeal to Franklin had not been weakened in this specific way, an appeal to the opinion of a person who was not commenting on the law being discussed would have been in the nature of the fallacy of *ad verecundiam*, in tending to prevent full discussion of the merits of the issue at hand. It also seems a reasonable presumption in view of Harper's position on the Sedition Act that he would have been proposing it even if Franklin had not made his comment, which brings out the fallacious and pretext-like nature of his argument.

Here is another point that Harper made:

> Mr. H. knew the liberty of the press had been carried to a very considerable extent in this country. He had frequently seen private character vilely calumniated; he had himself come in for a share of abuse, but he had always despised the base calumniators, believing that a man's propriety of conduct would always be sufficient to shield him against these slanders. When he saw the President of the United States and the Government of the Union defamed, he still despised them, and he believed also that the people were not affected by them, because he saw they did not rise in insurrection against the Government; and if they had not believed that all the things which were said respecting the Government were vile falsehoods, he should have thought the people the most wretched fools, had they not risen against it.
>
> Whilst this abuse was confined to certain newspapers in the United States, it excited in him, therefore, no alarm; but, when he heard a gentleman on the floor of this House, whose character and connexions gave him weight with the people, pronouncing an invective against the Government, and calling upon the people to rise against the law, the business put on a very serious appearance; he thought so, not because he should wish to have that gentleman muzzled (for he knew he had the liberty of uttering as much treason as he pleased, and that if his own sense of propriety and decorum was not sufficient to check him, there was no other check upon him,) but because this speech may have a very different effect from the filthy streams of certain newspapers; it may gain credit with the community, and produce consequences which all former abuse has failed to do. It is time, therefore, for the Government to take alarm; the long forbearance which it has shown ought to come to an end, since all its acts are represented in the vilest and foulest colors; and now they are sanctioned by the assertions of a person high in respectability (he meant as to his situation in life) and a law ought to pass to prevent such invitations as had been given to the people from producing their intended effects. It was for this reason that he wished a law to pass to punish treasonable and seditious writings. (*Debates* (1851a, 2102 f.))

Harper was saying that he was supporting the Sedition Act because of what a member of Congress had said in a Congressional debate. While Harper complimented the member as being "a person high in respectability," the logic of the argument would have been to ban reports of Congressional debates or, even though Harper disavowed this possibility, to extend the Sedition Act to apply to debates on the floor of the Congress.

Two Republican opponents of the Sedition Act, John Nicholas and Edward Livingston spoke next. Both made relatively brief remarks. Here is part of the record of Nicholas's speech:

> The people of this country are competent judges of their own interests, and he was desirous that the press should remain perfectly free to give them every information relative to them; and to restrict it, would be to create a suspicion that there is something in our measures which ought to be kept from the light. It was striking at the root of free republican Government, to restrict the use of speaking and writing. (*Debates* (1851a, 2104))

Nicholas was thus providing another echo of Republican speakers in the November 1794 debate, arguing the people should be the judges of their interests and that the press should remain free from legislative restrictions.

For his part, Livingston reacted to the speeches of both Allen, from Connecticut, and of Harper, from South Carolina:

> Mr. LIVINGSTON said, after receiving the chastisement of the gentleman from Connecticut on one cheek, he, like a good Christian, had turned the other to the gentleman from South Carolina, and received the stripes of both. He expressed his acknowledgment to these gentlemen, however, if not for their chastisement, for the insight which they have given the House into this bill. They have said, its design is not only to restrict the liberty of the press, which is secured by the Constitution, but the liberty of speech on this floor. (*Debates* (1851a, 2104))

Livingston's reaction to the *ad hominem* attacks was thus one of detachment and self-control.

He went on to raise an important and obvious objection to the proposed Sedition Act:

> The gentleman from South Carolina has said, that provided the law is clear and well defined, and the trial by jury is preserved, he knew of no law which could infringe the liberty of the press. If this be true, Congress might restrict all printing at once. We have, said he, nothing to do but to make the law precise, and then we may forbid a newspaper to be printed, and make it death for any man to attempt it!
>
> If this be the extent to which this bill goes, it is not only an abridgment of the liberty of the press, which the Constitution has said shall not be abridged; but it is a total annihilation of the press. (*Debates* (1851a, 2105))

The important point here is Livingston's reference to the First Amendment, expressly saying that "Congress shall make no law ... abridging the freedom of speech, or of the press." Livingston is thus claiming that the proposed act is unconstitutional.

Harrison Otis, an influential Federalist, spoke next. The report of his speech may be reproduced in full:

> Mr. OTIS supposed the opposition to this bill arose chiefly from prejudice, as gentlemen could not be so well acquainted with the bill from hearing it once read, as to say there are no parts of it which ought to become law. He had not nicely examined the merits of this bill, but he heard that it contained several important provisions, and he should certainly be opposed to a rejection of it without a perusal. To vote for such a motion, would be to say, we will not examine the bill; and yet he believed there was nothing in it contrary to the common law of the several States of the Union. (*Debates* (1851a, 2105))

In the last sentence of his statement Representative Otis linked the Sedition Act to the common law in effect in the different States by saying that "he believed there was nothing in it contrary to the common law of the several States of the Union." This might be seen under the label of the fallacy from precedent: what was being proposed had a precedent in several of the States and therefore it should be done at the Federal level. Such an argument ignores the difference between the two levels of government and may be intended to cut off debate on the content of the measure being contemplated and its nature at the Federal level. The argument as employed here is a fallacy from this point of view.

It is also worth noting that while Otis spoke of the common law of the several States of the Union, he did not make the claim that there was a common law at the Federal level.

Nathaniel Macon, a Republican, speaking next, pressed the Constitutional issue, originally raised by Livingston:

> No gentleman, in support of the bill, has gone into the Constitutional question; no one has shown what part of the Constitution will authorize the passage of a law like this. He believed none such could be adduced. (*Debates* (1851a, 2106))

He also questioned the necessity of a Federal law:

> The gentleman from Massachusetts (Mr. OTIS) has said, this bill is conformable to the common law. He knew persons might be prosecuted for a libel under the State Governments; but if this power exist in full force at present, what necessity can there be for this bill? (*Debates* (1851a, 2106))

Representative McDowell spoke next:

> Mr. MCDOWELL was in hopes that when the third article of the amendments to

the Constitution had been read, that the unconstitutionality of this bill would have been so evident, that it would have been rejected without debate.

Mr. McD. was sorry that the gentleman from Connecticut should have thought it necessary to have taken up so much of the time of the House by reading paragraphs from newspapers, which everybody had seen; but it might have been expected after the gentleman had taken so much pains to vilify and abuse the printer of one of the papers of this city, a citizen of respectable character and connexions, that he should have taken at least some notice of another, called the British printer, who boasts of being a subject of King George, and who is generally supposed to be in the pay of the British Minister—whose paper contains more libels and lies than any other in the United States, ... (*Debates* (1851a, 2106 f.))

McDowell thus kept up the Republican theme of reminding Federalists of the First Amendment. He also pointed out the highly selective and partisan nature of Allen's illustrations of newspaper excesses.

A later important speaker was Albert Gallatin, a leading Republican. One point he made was in response to Allen's early concern about a newspaper report about Gerry's mission to France:

... was there any thing criminal in that paragraph: It asserted that Mr. Gerry had powers sufficient to treat. The gentleman from Connecticut denies this to be true. Mr. G. would aver that it was an undeniable fact, as appears evidently from the documents now on the table. They showed that the powers given to the Envoys were joint and several. And, if Mr. Gerry had powers to treat, how could it be criminal to say that he might treat? Or supposing the writer of the paragraph to have said, that he believed Mr. Gerry would treat, could the opinion be charged with anything but being erroneous? When a paragraph of this nature was held out as criminal, what writings, what opinions, could escape the severity of the intended law, which did not coincide with the opinions, and which might counteract the secret views of a prevailing party? (*Debates* (1851a, 2108))

Gallatin also made another important point:

This bill and its supporters suppose, in fact, that whoever dislikes the measures of Administration and of a temporary majority in Congress, and shall either by speaking or writing, express his disapprobation and his want of confidence in the men now in power, is seditious, is an enemy, not of Administration, but of the Constitution, and is liable to punishment. That principle, Mr. G. said, was subversive of the principles of the Constitution itself. If you put the press under any restraint in respect to the measures of members of Government; if you thus deprive the people of the means of obtaining information of their conduct, you in fact render their right of electing nugatory; and this bill must be considered only as a weapon used by a party now in power, in order to perpetuate their authority and preserve their present places. (*Debates* (1851a, 2110))

Gallatin thus linked the necessity of a free press to the very existence of representative government.

The last speaker was Representative Kittera, a Federalist:

Mr. KITTERA said, gentlemen's arguments were at war with each other. On one side it is said, the bill is a violation of the Constitution; on the other, it is said to be founded on common law principles. If the latter is true, it may be wise and proper to pass this bill. It was wise in all Governments to have the people well informed with respect to crimes on common law principles. It was desirable on another count: It had lately been advanced as an opinion by law gentlemen in the Federal Courts, that those Courts have not a common law jurisdiction in criminal cases. If so, it is important to pass a bill on the subject. (*Debates* (1851a, 2113))

The noteworthy feature of these remarks is Kittera's hesitation and uncertainty about the jurisdiction of the Federal Government and the desire to clarify the position with the adoption of the Sedition Act.

At the end of the debate, the House of Representatives divided, and rejected the motion to reject the Sedition Act by a vote of 47 to 36. The vote was almost entirely on partisan lines, with Federalists voting not to reject the Act and with Republicans voting to reject it.

Summing Up

Assessing the debate of July 5, 1798 as a whole, it can be said that the Sedition Act was viewed by both Federalists and by Republicans, with unanimity, as limiting freedom of expression. Both the major Federalist speakers, Allen and Harper, stated this openly.

Federalist argumentation for the new act was at a fairly simple and unsophisticated level in this first debate: the claim that members of the Administration had been "shamefully" attacked in the press and that the new Act was needed to put a stop to such attacks was the main argument put forward.

At one point, indeed, Representative Allen indeed let slip the statement that "it is our business to wrest it [the press, J.R.] from them." This is a remarkably candid and blunt acknowledgement of a Federalist objective, of a type that is usually kept well hidden in political argumentation, because of its clearly partisan and discreditable nature.

There were not many other noteworthy arguments for the Sedition Act to emerge in this first debate. As noted, Otis suggested that "there was nothing in it contrary to the common law of the several States of the Union," conveniently disregarding the difference between the State and Federal levels of government. At the end of the debate, Kittera suggested that is was desirable to clarify the status of what he took to be a Federal common law of libel.

Federalist rhetoric was also often characterized by fallacies in this debate. Such fallacies were designed to close down discussion or to deflect it away from the merits or demerits of the measure being considered or to obscure the motives that Federalists had with the measure. A particularly prominent fallacy was *ad hominem,* with Federalists subjecting Representative Livingston, who had moved that the bill be rejected, to personal attacks. One form of attack was that of trying to apply a derogatory epithet to this Representative. Paradoxically, examples of derogatory epithets used by Republican newspapers to characterize Federalists were at the same time cited by Federalists as a reason for the Sedition Act.

Republican arguments against the introduction of the Sedition Act centered on the First Amendment from the beginning. Republican speaker after Republican speaker argued that the new Act violated the First Amendment.

Republican speakers, similarly to their counterparts in November 1794, also argued that the people and public opinion would be able to winnow out lies and slanders, and that legislation was an unsuitable means to this end.

Gallatin also made the point that if freedom of expression is restricted, the whole system of republican government becomes nugatory, since the people do not get the information on which to base a reasoned choice.

Overall, Republicans had a number of significant arguments against the Sedition Act, but Federalists failed to address them in this first debate.

The Debate of July 10, 1798

Turning now to the debate of July 10, 1798, it may be observed that the Act had now assumed its final form and the question was whether it should be passed. Some of the most influential Federalists and Republicans took part in the debate preceding the vote, and the purpose of this investigation is to examine the nature of arguments on the two sides.

The substantive part of the debate of July 10, 1798 was opened by John Nicholas of Virginia. He asked a pointed question:

> Mr. NICHOLAS rose, he said, to ask an explanation of the principles upon which the bill is founded. He confessed it was strongly impressed upon his mind, that it was not within the powers of the House to act upon this subject. He looked in vain amongst the enumerated powers given to Congress in the Constitution, for an authority to pass a law like the present; but he found what he considered as an express

prohibition against passing it. He found that, in order to quiet the alarms of the people of the United States with respect to the silence of the Constitution as to the liberty of the press, not being perfectly satisfied that the powers not vested in Congress remained with the people, that one of the first acts of this Government was to propose certain amendments to the Constitution, to put this matter beyond doubt, which amendments are now become a part of the Constitution. It is now expressly declared by that instrument, "that the powers not delegated to the United States by the Constitution, nor prohibited by it to the States, are reserved to the States respectively, or to the people;" and, also, "that Congress shall make no law abridging the freedom of speech, or of the press."

   Mr. N. asked whether this bill did not go to the abridgment of the freedom of speech and of the press? If it did not, he would be glad if gentlemen would define wherein the freedom of speech and of the press consists. (*Debates* (1851a, 2139 f.))

Nicholas was thus immediately back to the central Republican argument that the proposed Sedition Act was unconstitutional in view of the First Amendment. Nicholas added force to the argument by reproducing the language of the Amendment.

A further part of his speech is also worth considering:

   Mr. N. wished gentlemen, before they give a final vote on this bill, to consider its effects; and, if they do this, he thought they would consent to stop here. He desired them to reflect on the nature of our Government; that all its officers are elective, and that the people have no other means of examining their conduct but by means of the press, and an unrestrained investigation through them of the conduct of the Government. Indeed, the heart and life of a free Government, is a free press; take away this, and you take away its main support. You might as well say to the people, we, your Representatives, are faithful servants, you need not look into our conduct; we will keep our seats for a little longer time than that for which you have given them to us. To restrict the press, would be to destroy the elective principle, by taking away the information necessary to election, and there would be no difference between it and a total denial of the right of election, but in the degree of usurpation. (*Debates* (1851a, 2144))

Here Nicholas echoed Gallatin's point in the earlier debate, by arguing that to restrict the press "would be to destroy the elective principle."

A Federalist response to Nicholas came from Harrison Otis:

   The gentleman had caught an alarm on the first suggestion of a sedition bill, which had not yet subsided; and though the present bill is perfectly harmless, and contains no provision which is not practised upon under the laws of the several States in which gentlemen had been educated, and from which they had drawn most of their ideas of jurisprudence, yet the gentleman continues to be dissatisfied with it. (*Debates* (1851a, 2145))

The first point here involved a degree of the fallacy of *ad hominem*. The representation of Nicholas's concerns as resulting from an emotion that had possessed him and had not yet subsided focused on the person holding a certain opinion, rather than on the content of the opinion, and thus suggested the fallacy of *ad hominem*.

The second point in this part of Otis's speech was that the new law contained nothing new because all the provisions of the bill were already being practiced in the States.

This is a common type of argument used when trying to justify a new measure causing concern and to downplay the concern felt about it. It harks back to Otis's remark in the debate of July 5, 1798, and can be seen in the light of the fallacy from precedent. Otis was arguing that because what was being proposed had precedents in several States, it should be done at the Federal level. The use of the argument is fallacious in its aspect of cutting off debate on the nature of the measure at the Federal level.

In the further course of his remarks, Otis analyzed the Constitutional issue raised by Nicholas in this way:

The objections of the gentleman from Virginia, he believed, might be reduced to two inquiries. In the first place, had the Constitution given Congress cognizance over the offences described in this bill prior to the adoption of the amendments to the Constitution? and, if Congress had that cognizance before that time, have those amendments taken it away? (*Debates* (1851a, 2145 f.))

With respect to the first question, Otis lost little time in answering it in the affirmative:

With respect to the first question, it must be allowed that every independent Government has a right to preserve and defend itself against injuries and outrages which endanger its existence; for, unless it has this power, it is unworthy the name of a free Government, and must either fall or be subordinate to some other protection. Now some of the offences delineated in the bill are of this description. (*Debates* (1851a, 2146))

The argument here might be characterized as one of *ad definitionem*: a free government has the right, by definition, to preserve itself against some of the offences contained in the Sedition Act. Such a definitional argument, as used here, would, if accepted, close down debate on the nature of the offences in question and on the question of whether it is reasonable to guard against them by a Federal law, and in this light the argument may here be seen as a fallacy of *ad definitionem*.

In the extract quoted above, Otis said that "some of the offences delineated in the bill are of this description." However, he continued:

> It has been said by the gentleman that the Constitution has specified the only crimes that are cognizable under it; but other crimes had been made penal at an early period of the Government, by express statute, to which no exception has been taken. For example, stealing public records, perjury, obstructing the officers of justice, bribery in a Judge, and even a contract to give a bribe, (which last was a restraint upon the liberty of writing and speaking,) were all punishable, and why? Not because they are described in the Constitution, but because they are crimes against the United States— because laws against them are necessary to carry other laws into effect; because they tend to subvert the Constitution. The same reasons applied to the offences mentioned in the bill.
>
> Mr. OTIS contended that this construction of the Constitution was abundantly supported by the act for establishing the Judicial Courts. That act, in describing certain powers of the District Court, contains this remarkable expression: "saving to suitors in all cases the right of a common law remedy, where the common law was competent to give it." He could not tell whence this competency was derived, unless from the Constitution; nor did he perceive how this competency applied to civil and not to criminal cases. (*Debates* (1851a, 2147))

The argument here may be seen in the light of the fallacy from precedent: because an act had been passed that mentioned common law competency and because the power to pass such an act must have been derived from the Constitution, the Constitution also gave a warrant to pass laws regarding the offences included in the Sedition Act.

Otis proceeded in his argument:

> It was, therefore, most evident to his mind, that the Constitution of the United States, prior to the amendments that have been added to it, secured to the National Government the cognizance of all the crimes enumerated in the bill, and it only remained to be considered whether those amendments divested it of this power. The amendment quoted by the gentleman from Virginia is in these words: "Congress shall make no law abridging the freedom of speech and of the press." The terms "freedom of speech and of the press," he supposed, were a phraseology perfectly familiar in the jurisprudence of every State, and of a certain and technical meaning. It was a mode of expression which we had borrowed from the only country in which it had been tolerated, and he pledged himself to prove that the construction which he should give to those terms, should be consonant not only to the laws of that country, but to the laws and judicial decisions of many of the States composing the Union. This freedom, said Mr. O., is nothing more than the liberty of writing, publishing, and speaking,

one's thoughts, under the condition of being answerable to the injured party, whether it be the Government or an individual, for false, malicious, and seditious expressions, whether spoken or written; and the liberty of the press is merely an exemption from all previous restraints. In support of this doctrine, he quoted *Blackstone's Commentaries,* under the head of libels, and read an extract to prove that in England, formerly, the press was subject to a licenser; and that this restraint was afterward removed, by which means the freedom of the press was established. (*Debates* (1851a, 2147 f.))

The first sentence is a remarkably straightforward statement of Federalist thinking regarding the powers of the Federal Government if there had not been a Bill of Rights.

The passage is also significant and noteworthy for a number of other reasons. It is interesting from the point of view of fallacy theory. Harrison Otis took up the concepts of "freedom of the speech and of the press," and argued that they have a "certain and technical meaning." This way of putting it suggests that Otis was conceding that the concepts might have been understood in a different way without his definition. However, he took the key words of the debate and defined them in a way that suited his argumentative purpose, trying to shut off further debate on the issue. This might be viewed as an instance of the fallacy of *ad definitionem.*

Otis derived the definition that he proposed from an authority, *Blackstone's Commentaries.* As far as the present investigator has been able to determine, this is the first and only explicit reference to *Blackstone's Commentaries* in the Congressional debates of July 5 and July 10, 1798. Blackstone was a British Tory, who wrote and published his book in Great Britain in the middle of the eighteenth century, before American independence. Here is his view of what liberty of the press meant:

The liberty of the press is indeed essential to the nature of a free state: but this consists in laying no *previous* restraints upon publications, and not in freedom from censure for criminal matter when published. Every freeman has an undoubted right to lay what sentiments he pleases before the public: to forbid this, is to destroy the freedom of the press: but if he publishes what is improper, mischievous, or illegal, he must take the consequences for his own temerity. (Blackstone [1769] 1966, 151 f.), the emphasis in the original)

Harrison Otis thus did not misrepresent the Blackstonian view, as presented in *Blackstone's Commentaries.* However, it is worth noting how he went on immediately after the extract above:

He would not, however, dwell upon the law of England, the authority of which it might suit the convenience of gentlemen to question; ... (*Debates* (1851a, 2148))

This is an interesting statement from this leading Federalist politician. It indicates that in July 1798 he characterized Blackstone's view as "the law of England" and that he did not wish to argue that Blackstone's English view of the concept of freedom of expression was necessarily applicable in the United States at the Federal level.

Instead, Otis sought to argue that there were some State Constitutions with language that in his view was of relevance to the issue of whether the Sedition Act was compatible with the First Amendment:

> To begin with New Hampshire: In the Bill of Rights of that State, it is declared, "That the liberty of the press is essential to the security of freedom in a State; it ought, therefore, to be inviolably preserved." By an act passed in February, 1791, subsequent to the adoption of that Constitution, "any person of the age of fourteen and upward, making and publishing a lie or libel, tending to the defamation of any person, is liable on conviction to a fine," &c. (*Debates* (1851a, 2148))

Next, Otis proceeded to list some other States which had both a provision for freedom of the press and a law of libel, and he argued that "in all these instances, it is clearly understood, that to punish licentiousness and sedition is not a restraint or abridgment of the freedom of speech or of the press" (*Debates* (1851a, 2149)).

Otis's argument can be seen to be in the nature of a fallacy, most appropriately that of the fallacy from analogy:

> The right thing to do is for an individual State Government to have enacted both a law for protecting freedom of the press and a law of libel.

> The Federal Government is similar to a State Government.

> The right thing to do is for the Federal Government to enact both a law for protecting freedom of the press and a law of libel.

However, the State and Federal levels of government are two distinct levels of government, each with its own functions, characteristics and powers, and the analogy may break down.

There is also a more specific difference that Otis did not notice or did not wish to notice. Here is again the language that he cited from the Bill of Rights of New Hampshire:

> "That the liberty of the press is essential to the security of freedom in a State; it ought, therefore, to be inviolably preserved."

Compare this with the language of the First Amendment:

Congress shall make no law ... abridging the freedom of speech, or of the press;

There is a perceptible difference in the language of the two laws. The New Hampshire Bill of Rights is less specific, more in the nature of a declaration or a philosophical statement. The "shall" of the Federal law is more forceful than the "ought to" of the New Hampshire law, but more importantly, the Federal Bill of Rights places a clearly defined and pointed prohibition on the power of the Legislature, by specifically prohibiting Congress from making any law abridging freedom of speech. The State Constitutions cited by Otis did not all have the precise form of the New Hampshire Constitution that Otis cited first, but it was the case that the language of the Federal Bill of Rights was more specific and pointed than the language of State Constitutions in placing a well defined restriction on the power of the Legislature. The difference undermines the analogy that Otis sought to establish between the two levels of government.

At the same time, Otis's argument brought out an important property of the Sedition Act, namely, that it was an attempt to enact a Federal law of libel, with special reference to Federal officials.

In the further course of his remarks, Otis said in part:

There are sixteen Legislatures in the United States, in which all the measures of Government are open to investigation. There are two Houses of Congress, in which every accusation and suspicion may have free vent, wherein our jealousies and prejudices may be uttered without restraint, and every man will still be at liberty to print and speak at pleasure; but he must be prepared to prove those charges which bring disgrace upon his fellow-citizens. No reasonable being can desire a greater latitude than this. (*Debates* (1851a, 2150))

Otis's remark here harks back to a tradition introduced by the English Bill of Rights of 1688, which gave the Legislature a special status with respect to freedom of expression, for it had the provision "that the freedom of speech and debates or proceedings in parliament ought not to be impeached or questioned in any court or place out of parliament" (Stephenson and Marcham (1972, 601)).

Perhaps the most revealing word in the passage is the word "still," signifying an admission on Otis's part that in his conception, the Sedition Act was designed to restrict freedom of the press from what it would have been in the absence of the Sedition Act.

Addressing his remarks to Representative Nicholas specifically, Otis went on to say:

He urges further that, even in Great Britain, Parliament has never made laws to restrain censorious remarks upon its measures; but in Great Britain, Government is more able to protect itself, and, if the gentleman pleases, he may add, it is less deserving of protection. It should be remembered, too, that the esteem and confidence of the people is of less consequence to a British Parliament, than it is to an American Congress; and, moreover, that libels as well against Parliament, as other bodies of men, are offences at common law. (*Debates* (1851a, 2150))

Otis claimed here that the American Congress was more deserving of protection than the British Parliament. This might be called a fallacy *ad superbiam,* or of self-elevation.

Representative Macon, a Republican, spoke after Representative Otis, in opposition to the Sedition Act. One of his points concerned the Republican theme of constitutionality: "that it was never understood that prosecutions for libels could take place under the General Government; but that they must be carried on in the State courts, as the Constitution gave no power to Congress to pass laws on the subject" (*Debates* (1851a, 2151)).

Edward Livingston again spoke against the proposed Act. He said in part:

This privilege [the liberty of speech and of the press, JR] is connected with another dear and valuable privilege—the liberty of conscience. What is liberty of conscience? Gentlemen may tomorrow establish a national religion agreeably to the opinion of a majority of this House, on the ground of an uniformity of worship being more consistent with public happiness than a diversity of worship. The doing of this is not less forbidden than the act which the House are about to do. (*Debates* (1851a, 2153))

Livingston was perhaps indulging here in the fallacy of the slippery slope. This fallacy "occurs where one party warns a respondent that if he takes some contemplated course of action, it would trigger a whole series of ensuing events, unleashing an irresistible force that would result in some particularly horrible outcome for the respondent" (Walton (1995, 54)). The fallacy comes to mind because Livingston was dwelling on the prospect of an ensuing calamity, rather than focusing on the nature of the issue at hand.

In the further course of his remarks Livingston came to articulate an important legal and Constitutional principle regarding the question of what freedom of speech ought to mean:

But, it is said this Government is liable to suffer abuse of the worst kind; the worst motives may be attributed to it, the most false statements made with respect to its conduct, and no hand can be held out to protect it. For his own part, he believed there ought to be no such power. He believed every independent Government was equal to the protection of its private or public character; but when gentlemen speak of slanders against the Government, he knew of no such thing. (*Debates* (1851a, 2154))

Livingston thus expressed the position that there should be no such thing as a slander against a government. Charges against the government, according to him, should be decided by the force of reason, and not by a criminal trial:

> We are charged, for instance, with passing an unconstitutional act—with violating our oaths. What answer is it proposed we should make to the charge? We are not to disprove the fact, and let the public judge between us, but we are immediately to prosecute the man who makes the charge. You may, by thus acting, establish error as soon as truth; you put them both on the same footing; you crush them by force of arms, and not by the force of reason. (*Debates* (1851a, 2154))

In his statement Livingston articulated a philosophical position on the freedom of the press that was pregnant with meaning for the future.

Albert Gallatin, a Republican, was the next speaker to make a substantive speech. He characterized the purpose of the proponents of the Act by saying that it was a law "intended by its supporters for the sole purpose of enacting into a law of the United States the common law of libels" (*Debates* (1851a, 2157)). He went on, referring to Otis:

> The gentleman from Massachusetts himself, by his efforts to obtain this law, had shown that he did not believe that the courts could act in the case of libels, without the assistance of a law; and every gentleman who had spoken in favor of this bill had explicitly declared, as his opinion, that the Federal Courts had no jurisdiction whatever over offences at common law. The fact was, that the gentleman from Massachusetts, although he had at first stated the question correctly, by saying that it was sufficient to prove that the power of passing this bill was given by the Constitution, had afterwards altogether forgotten his own position—the position which it was incumbent upon him to prove—and had attempted to establish another point, unconnected with the first. The question was not whether the Courts of the United States had, without this law, the power to punish libels, but whether, supposing they had not the power, Congress had that of giving them this jurisdiction—whether Congress were vested by the Constitution with the authority of passing this bill? (*Debates* (1851a, 2157 f.))

Gallatin was thus again emphasizing the constitutional question relating the powers of Congress. He went on to provide an important perspective on the reasoning behind the First Amendment:

> Mr. G. said that he had heretofore considered the Constitution as it originally stood, and that it must be evident that no law against libels could be passed by Congress, unless it was under color of carrying into effect some other distinct power vested in

them. However improbable such an attempt might have appeared, the bill now under discussion justified the suspicions of those who, at the time of the adoption of the Constitution, had apprehended that the sense of that generally expressed clause might be distorted for that purpose. It was in order to remove these fears, that the amendment, which declares that Congress shall pass no law abridging the freedom of speech or the liberty of the press, was proposed and adopted—an amendment which was intended as an express exception to any supposed general power of *passing laws,* &c., vested in Congress by the other clause. The sense, in which he and his friends understood this amendment, was that Congress could not pass any law to punish any real or supposed abuse of the press. (*Debates* (1851a, 2159 f.))

Gallatin developed another practical point arising from the nature of political journalism:

It was true that, so far as related merely to facts, a man would be acquitted by proving that what he asserted was true. But the bill was intended to punish solely writings of a political nature, libels against the Government, the President, or either branch of the Legislature; and it was well known that writings, containing animadversions on public measures, almost always contained not only facts but opinions. And how could the truth of opinions be proven by evidence? If an individual thinking, as he himself did, that the present bill was unconstitutional, and that it had been intended, not for the public good, but solely for party purposes, should avow and publish his opinion, and if the Administration thought fit to prosecute him for that supposed individual offence, would a jury, composed of the friends of that Administration, hesitate much in declaring the opinion ungrounded, or, in other words, false and scandalous, and its publication malicious? And by what kind of argument or evidence, in the present temper of parties, could the accused convince them that his opinion was true? (*Debates* (1851a, 2162))

Gallatin thus pointed out that there was a distinction between facts and opinions, and provided an illustration of how difficult it would be to "prove" opinions. Gallatin's implication is that the consequence of the Sedition Act would be considerably to restrict the expression of opinions and to narrow down the range of political debate.

Robert Harper, a Federalist, was the next speaker in the debate. In his speech, he made a point that had been conspicuous by its absence from Federalist arguments for the Sedition Act in the two debates up to this point. He noted that the country had done without the Sedition Act for nine years and asked the important question of what had changed. Here is part of what he said:

The change, in his opinion, consisted in this: that heretofore we had been at peace, and were now on the point of being driven into a war with a nation which openly boasts of its party among us, and its "diplomatic skill," as the most effectual means of paralyzing our efforts, and bringing us to its own terms. (*Debates* (1851a, 2164 f.))

Here is how Harper characterized the nature of the Sedition Act in relation to practices relating to freedom of speech in the first nine years of the Republic:

It was honorable for the Government, Mr. HARPER said, that it had existed for nine years, in safety, without such a law as this; and he still hoped that even now, there would be little or no occasion for enforcing the law should it pass, but of this he was far from being certain. The coat of mail which Congress was about to provide in this law, might turn away the point of some dagger aimed at the heart of the Government, and in that case it would, he said, be matter of rejoicing that the bill had passed. Should no such case occur, then, like a sword, which there has been no occasion to draw, it will have done no harm. (*Debates* (1851a, 2165))

The comparisons here, with the Sedition Act represented as a coat of mail or a sword, make clear that the Act was seen by this leading Federalist as intended to restrict what was to be permitted for the press.

In the further course of his remarks, Harper gave his take on the question of the relation of the First Amendment and the Sedition Act:

In the other objection, he admitted that there was more plausibility; the objection founded on that part of the Constitution which provides that "Congress shall pass no law to abridge the liberty of speech or of the press." He held this to be one of the most sacred parts of the Constitution, one by which he would stand the longest, and defend with the greatest zeal. But to what, he asked, did this clause amount? Did this liberty of the press include sedition and licentiousness? Did it authorize persons to throw, with impunity, the most violent abuse upon the President and both Houses of Congress? Was this what gentlemen meant by the liberty of the press? As well might it be said that the liberty of action implied the liberty of assault, trespass, or assassination. Every man possessed the liberty of action; but if he used this liberty to the detriment of others, by attacking their persons or destroying their property, he became liable to punishment for this licentious abuse of his liberty. The liberty of the press stood on precisely the same footing. (*Debates* (1851a, 2167))

The fallacy of false analogy may be invoked here. Harper's argument is the following:

The right thing to do to prevent people from abusing their freedom of action to engage in assault, trespass, and assassination is to restrict their freedom of action.

The abuses of the freedom of expression are similar to the abuses of the freedom of action.

The right thing to do to prevent people from abusing their freedom of expression is to restrict their freedom of expression.

The weakness of the argument is in the presumed similarity of the two types of abuses. The point has been well addressed by James Morton Smith:

According to Harper's analogy, there could be no legal difference between a physical assault and a verbal attack—between saying "I'll punch you in the face" and actually striking a person. The analogy placed the spoken word on the same footing with the fatal finality of assassination and made shooting off at the mouth a crime equivalent to that of shooting off a gun in order to murder a person. Harper completely overlooked the fact that whatever damage is inflicted by physical action cannot be undone but only punished, while erroneous and even false views propagated by speech and the press can be rebutted by similar methods. Insults may be rectified by apology, and in the last resort, civil, and even criminal, libel suits can be instituted in the state courts. (Smith (1956, 139))

After Harper's speech the House of Representatives divided, and by a majority of 44 to 41 it passed the Sedition Act. The vote was largely on partisan lines, with Federalists in favor and Republicans opposed.

Summing Up

It was observed above how the theme of Republican speakers in the debate of July 5, 1798 was what they took to be the unconstitutionality of the Sedition Act, in view of the First Amendment. This theme continued to be the dominant one for Republicans in the debate of July 10, 1798.

The argument was not addressed by Federalists in the debate of July 5, 1798, but in the debate of July 10, 1798, two leading Federalists, Harrison Otis and Robert Harper, both attempted to address the issue. Otis invoked *Blackstone's Commentaries,* but immediately dismissed Blackstone as an authority by saying that "he would not ... dwell upon the law of England, the authority of which it might suit the convenience of gentlemen to question" (*Debates* (1851a, 2143)).

Instead, Otis proceeded to argue that there were States that had Constitutions with provisions to protect freedom of the press and that these States also had laws against libel and against the libeling of State officials. However, in the debate the issue came back again and again to the First Amendment, with its specific provision against Congress enacting any law abridging freedom of speech, and Republicans continued to hold the view that the Sedition Act was unconstitutional, given this specific provision of the First Amendment.

Harper's attempted defense of the presumed power of Congress to enact a law of the type of the Sedition Act was less subtle than Otis's. It consisted in attempting to argue that a verbal assault is the same as a physical assault. The analogy breaks down, for instance as regards the way in which the two kinds of assault may be rectified, as noted by James Morton Smith.

What Federalists did not attempt to do in the debates of July 5 and July 10, 1798 was to claim the existence of a common law of libels at the Federal level. At the end of the debate of July 5, 1798 Representative Kittera, a Federalist, had raised the question about a putative common law of libels, arguing that the Sedition Act would and should clarify the question. In the debate of July 10, 1798 there were references to State laws, but there was a conspicuous lack of reference to the issue of a putative common law of libels at the Federal level. The issue was a live one at the time of the debates, as noted in the introductory section of this chapter. However, in the debates Federalists, including Otis and Kittera, shied away from asserting that there existed a common law of libels at the Federal level.

Instead, in the debates of July 5 and July 10, 1798 Federalists made clear their desire to impose restrictions on what was permissible for the press. Indeed in these debates both Republicans and Federalists shared the position that the Sedition Act, if enacted, would impose restrictions on what could be published with impunity. It can thus be said on the basis of this unanimity of views that the Sedition Act was conceived by Federalists with the aim of limiting freedom of expression — or to achieve "genuine" freedom of speech, as some Federalists were fond of putting it as early as in 1794 — and that this was also the way that the Sedition Act was perceived by those who opposed it.

The Sedition Act was a brainchild of the Federalist party, and their representatives with very rare exceptions supported it. Of course, there were nuances even among Federalists, and historians have recorded the special zeal of certain Federalists to use the Act to prosecute their Republican opponents, who were a minority in Congress and in opposition at the Federal level at that time. The Act was conceived with the aim of limiting freedom of expression, and it certainly achieved the aim of subjecting Republicans to criminal prosecutions, as has been detailed be historians. Indeed among the victims was even a sitting Republican Congressman, Matthew Lyon, who was jailed for several months for expressing sentiments critical of the Adams administration (see Rudanko (2001)).

Notes

1. The text of the proposed law that would become the Sedition Act had the following form on July 5, 1798, according to the *Debates*:

[This bill provides, that if any persons shall unlawfully combine or conspire together, with intent to oppose any measure of the Government of the United States, or to impede the operation of any law, or to intimidate or prevent any person holding an office under the Government from exercising his trust. And if any person shall, by writing, printing, or speaking, threaten such officer with any damage to his character, person, or estate, or shall counsel, advise, or attempt to procure any insurrection, riot, &c., whether such attempt shall have the desired effect, or not, he shall be deemed guilty of a high misdemeanor, and punished by a fine, on conviction, not exceeding $5,000, and by imprisonment not less than six months, nor exceeding five years. And if any person shall, by any libellous or scandalous writing, printing, publishing, or speaking, traduce or defame the Legislature of the United States, by seditious or inflammatory declarations or expressions, with intent to create a belief in the citizens thereof, that the said Legislature in enacting any law, was induced thereto by motives hostile to the Constitution, or liberties, and happiness of the people thereof: or shall, in manner aforesaid, traduce or defame the President of the United States, or any Court, or Judge thereof, by declarations tending to criminate their motives in any official transaction, the persons so offending, being convicted, shall be punished by a fine not exceeding $2,000, and by imprisonment not exceeding two years.] (*Debates* (1851a, 2093))

2. The House of Representatives, sitting as a Committee of the Whole, made some major revisions to the text of the Act on Monday, July 9, 1798. Among the changes adopted was one proposed by Representative Harper permitting truth to be used as a defense in prosecutions brought under the Sedition Act.

Chapter 8

Change in Federalist Arguments: the Report of February 25, 1799

Introduction

The Sedition Act was passed by the Federalist majority in Congress and signed into law by President Adams in July 1798. Regarding the nature of the Act, it may be noted that as amended by the House of Representatives, it included some provisions that were claimed by Federalists to ameliorate its effects, including the provision that truth could be used in evidence in prosecutions under the Act. (The text of the Act was given at the beginning of chapter 7.) Here is a summary of these potentially ameliorating provisions:

> ... provisions were inserted by which truth was admitted as a defense in cases of slander and libel, proof of malicious intent was required, the jury was permitted to determine questions of law as well of fact, and limits were fixed upon the amount of the fine and term of imprisonment that could be imposed. In these respects, the Sedition Act was an improvement over the common law, by which, in case of libel, truth was no defense, the judge decided upon matters of intent, the jury was confined to questions of fact, and punishment was left to the discretion of the court. (Miller (1997, 579))

However, the potentially ameliorating provisions turned out to have little or no practical significance in the implementation of the Sedition Act. Here is a summary of how Act operated:

> ... these safeguards to the rights of the individual proved, in the actual execution of the law, to be of little avail. Judges and juries were usually biased against defendants and, owing to the rulings of the judges, truth was ineffective as a defense. As a result, the

Sedition Act bore out the Republicans' fears that it would be used to destroy freedom of speech and of the press. (Miller (1997, 579))

The present author discussed some aspects of a notorious prosecution under the Sedition Act, that against the sitting Republican Congressman Matthew Lyon, in Rudanko (2001, chapter 5). A number of leading Republican journalists were likewise prosecuted under the Act (Miller (1997, 580)).

As noted in the previous chapter, the major debates on the Sedition Act took place on July 5 and July 10, 1798 in the House of Representatives. As was seen, it was the constant theme of Republicans to argue that the proposed Sedition Act was unconstitutional in view of the First Amendment. Federalists did not have a coherent or principled answer to this charge in the debate of July 5, 1798. Instead, they pointed to what they viewed as excesses of the press and indeed engaged in *ad hominem* attacks directed at a newspaper and even at a Republican member of the House of Representatives.

As also noted, five days later, on July 10, 1798 Federalists did have an answer of a kind to the Republican charge that the First Amendment rendered the Sedition Act unconstitutional. Or more accurately, they had two answers. Two major Federalists, Harrison Otis and Robert Harper, spoke in the debate at length and each of them had a response. Otis brought up the Blackstonian interpretation of the freedom of the press, which "consists in laying no *previous* restraints upon publications" (Blackstone ([1769] 1966, 151 f., the emphasis in the original). "Every freeman," as Blackstone went on, "has an undoubted right to lay what sentiments he pleases before the public ... but if he publishes what is improper, mischievous, or illegal, he must take the consequence of his own temerity."

However, Otis immediately dismissed Blackstone as an authority. It is also worth emphasizing that neither he nor Harper argued that there was a common law of seditious libel at the Federal level in existence, in the absence of the Sedition Act. What Otis did argue was that State Constitutions had provisions both for protecting the freedom of the press and provisions against libel and that it was "clearly understood, that to punish licentiousness and sedition is not a restraint or abridgment of the freedom of speech or of the press" (*Debates* (1851a, 2149)). As noted, the analogy was undermined by the pointed language of the First Amendment.

For his part, Harper argued — fallaciously, it was suggested — that indulging in abusive language was the same as engaging physical assault or even assassination, and therefore it ought to be prohibited.

For their part, Republicans continued to insist in the debate of July 10, 1789 that the proposed Sedition Act violated the First Amendment.

In spite of the continuing sharp disagreement over the merits and the constitutionality of the Sedition Act, there was one fundamental point on which both Republicans and Federalists agreed in the debates of July 5, and July 10,

1798. This was the basic fact that the Sedition Act meant introducing a more restrictive practice on what was permissible in the press. Harper made the point explicit by saying that "it was honorable for the Government ... that it had existed for nine years, in safety, without such a law as this" and that "the coat of mail which Congress was about to provide in this law, might turn away the point of some dagger aimed at the heart of the Government" (*Debates* (1851a, 2165). It is also recalled that he raised the question of what change rendered the new law necessary and answered his question "that heretofore we had been at peace, and were now on a point of being driven into a war ..." (*Debates* (1851a, 2164)).

The unanimity on the point that the Sedition Act was intended to introduce restrictions on the press is linked to the assumption, which was also apparently shared by Republicans and Federalists in the debates of July 5, and July 10, 1798, that there was no common law of seditious libel at the Federal level. However, it did not take long for there to be a major shift in the Federalist position regarding the rationale for the Sedition Act. The purpose of this chapter is to examine aspects of a Committee Report submitted to the House on February 25, 1799 that revealed this shift.

The Report of February 1799

On February 25, 1799 the House of Representatives considered a report on the Alien and Sedition Acts, prepared by a select committee. Even though this is not explicitly stated in the record, it is safe to assume that the Report represented the view of the Federalist majority. This is a reasonable assumption to make because even though the debate that followed the presentation of the Report was brief, with Federalists seeking to curtail debate, Republican speakers criticized the Report. The debate is not discussed here, but the most salient segment of the Report deserves to be quoted in full.

The Report was structured to answer objections to the Alien and Sedition Acts, with individual objections formulated point by point in the Report. This is the way the criticism against the Sedition Act based on the First Amendment was phrased in the Report:

> It is objected to this act, in the second place, that it is expressly contrary to that part of the Constitution which declares, that "Congress shall make no law respecting an establishment of religion, or prohibiting the free exercise thereof, or abridging the liberty of the press." The act in question is said to be an "abridgment of the liberty of the press," and therefore unconstitutional. (*Debates* (1851a, 2988))

Here is how the Report deals with this objection:

To this it is answered, in the first place, that the liberty of the press consists not in a license for every man to publish what he pleases without being liable to punishment, if he should abuse this license to the injury of others, but in a permission to publish, without previous restraint, whatever he may think proper, being answerable to the public and individuals, for any abuse of this permission to their prejudice. In like manner, as the liberty of speech does not authorize a man to speak malicious slanders against his neighbor, nor the liberty of action justify him in going, by violence, into another man's house, or in assaulting any person whom he may meet in the streets. In the several States the liberty of the press has always been understood in this manner, and no other; and the Constitution of every State which has been framed and adopted since the Declaration of Independence, asserts "the liberty of the press;" while in several, if not all, their laws provide for the punishment of libellous publications, which would be a manifest absurdity and contradiction, if the liberty of the press meant to publish any and everything, without being amenable to the laws for the abuse of this license. According to this just, legal, and universally admitted definition of "the liberty of the press," a law to restrain its licentiousness, in publishing false, scandalous, and malicious libels against the Government, cannot be considered "an abridgment" of its "liberty."

It is answered, in the second place, that the liberty of the press did never extend, according to the laws of any State, or of the United States, or of England, from whence our laws are derived, to the publication of false, scandalous, and malicious writings against the Government, written or published with intent to do mischief, such publications being unlawful, and punishable in every State; from whence it follows, undeniably, that a law to punish seditious and malicious publications, is not an abridgment of the liberty of the press, for it would be a manifest absurdity to say, that a man's liberty was abridged by punishing him for doing that which he never had a liberty to do.

It is answered, thirdly, that the act in question cannot be unconstitutional, because it makes nothing penal that was not penal before, and gives no new powers to the court, but is merely declaratory of the common law, and useful for rendering that law more generally known, and more easily understood. This cannot be denied, it if be admitted, as it must be, that false, scandalous, and malicious libels against the Government of the country, published with intent to do mischief, are punishable by the common law; for, by the 2nd section of the 3rd article of the Constitution, the judicial power of the United States is expressly extended to all offences arising under the Constitution. By the Constitution, the Government of the United States is established, for many important objects, as the Government of the country; and libels against the Government, therefore, are offences arising under the Constitution, and, consequently, are punishable at common law, by the courts of the United States. The act, indeed, is so far from having extended the law and the power of the court, that it has abridged both, and has enlarged instead of abridging the liberty of the press; for, at common law, libels against the Government might be punished with fine and imprisonment at the discretion of the court, whereas the act limits the fine to two thousand dollars, and the imprisonment to two years; and it also allows the party accused to give the truth in evidence for his justification, which, by the common law, was expressly forbidden.

And, lastly, it is answered, that had the Constitution intended to prohibit Congress from legislating at all on the subject of the press, which is the construction whereon the objections to this law are founded, it would have used the same expressions as in that part of the clause which relates to religion and religious tests; whereas, the words are wholly different: "Congress," says the Constitution, (amendment 3rd), "shall make no law respecting an establishment of religion or prohibiting the free exercise thereof, or abridging the freedom of speech or of the press." Here it is manifest that the Constitution intended to prohibit Congress from legislating at all on the subject of religious establishments, and the prohibition is made in the most express terms. Had the same intention prevailed respecting the press, the same expressions would have been used, and Congress would have been "prohibited from passing any law respecting the press." They are not, however, "prohibited" from legislating at all on the subject, but merely from abridging the liberty of the press. It is evident they may legislate respecting the press, may pass laws for its regulation, and to punish those who pervert it into an engine of mischief, provided those laws do not abridge its liberty. Its liberty, according to the well known and universally admitted definition, consists in permission to publish, without previous restraint upon the press, but subject to punishment afterwards for improper publications. A law, therefore, to impose previous restraint upon the press, and not one to inflict punishment on wicked and malicious publications, would be a law to abridge the liberty of the press, and, as such, unconstitutional. (*Debates* (1851a, 2989 f.))

Some parts of this key segment of the Report are noteworthy for speculative or hair-splitting argumentation, including the speculation about how the provision about freedom of speech might have been phrased. However, the lengthy quotation is worth considering because it sheds light on continuity and change in the Federalist position on the Sedition Act from what it was in July 1798.

Regarding continuity, it is observed that Robert Harper's analogy, from July 1798, between a verbal and a physical assault is featured in the first answer. Similarly, Harrison Otis's earlier argument that State Constitutions had contained provisions for freedom of the press and for the punishment of libels and that this had not been interpreted as an abridgment of the liberty of the press is also found in the first answer. As noted in the previous chapter, both arguments were fallacious.

Such elements of continuity in the Report do not disguise a remarkable and indeed extraordinary shift in the Federalist approach to the Sedition Act in comparison with the position of July 1798. There is no talk now of the Federalist desire "to wrest it [the press, J.R.] from Republicans," as Allen had put it in the debate of July 5, 1798. That blunt statement may have been something that slipped from Allen inadvertently in an unguarded moment, and its exclusion from the Report is no surprise.

A more notable omission is the failure of the Federalist majority now to give any attention to the point that Robert Harper made in the debate of July 10, 1798 about it being "honorable for the Government ... that it had existed for nine years, in safety, without such a law as this" (*Debates* (1851a, 2165)). Nor did the Report now attach any importance to the point that Harper made about a change of circumstances that, as he alleged, had made the Sedition Act necessary, viz. that they "were now on the point of being driven into a war ..." (*Debates* (1851a, 2164)). Harper's point in support of the Sedition Act was of a contingent nature, and as such, it did not fit the Report of February 1799, where the argumentation took on a more timeless quality, not contingent on the circumstances of any particular point in time.

Another important change in the Federalist position deserves attention here. This is the claim in the Report that there existed a common law of seditious libel at the Federal level, independently of the Sedition Act. In the debate of July 5, 1798 the question concerning the existence of such a law had been raised by Representative John Kittera, who was a Federalist. As noted in the previous chapter, he had expressed considerable uncertainty about the issue. There was now no uncertainty in the Report: "... libels against the Government ... are punishable at common law, by the courts of the United States" (*Debates* (1851a, 2989)).

Proceeding, then, from the presumption that there was a common law of seditious libel in operation at the Federal level in the United States, the Report made this important claim:

> The act, indeed, is so far from having extended the law and the power of the court, that it has abridged both, and has enlarged instead of abridging the liberty of the press; ... (*Debates* (1851a, 2989)

The statement represents an extraordinary turnaround in the Federalist position on the rationale for the Sedition Act and in their characterization of the nature of the Act. As noted in the examination of the debates of July 5 and 10, 1798, there was a consensus, shared by both Republican and Federalist speakers in the debates, that the purpose of the Sedition Act was to restrict what can be published in the press with impunity. However, the opposite was now claimed by the Federalist authors of the Report only some seven months later. One of the images at that earlier time had been of the Sedition Act being a "coat of mail" that "might turn away the point of some dagger aimed at the heart of the Government" (*Debates* (1851a, 2165)). By contrast, it was now claimed by Federalists that the Act extended, instead of abridging, freedom of speech. This was a major change in the public position of Federalists, executed within the short space of some seven months. The change illustrates the flexibility of Federalist rhetoric in their eagerness to justify the Sedition Act. The question of how many Federalists genuinely and sincerely believed their own official argument merits further investigation.

Chapter 9

Defining Freedom of Speech: Madison's Report of 1800

Introduction

The previous chapter provided the Federalist position on the rationale for the Sedition Act, as formulated in the Report of February 1799. The new position represented an extraordinary turnaround from the position of the debates of July 1798: in July 1798 the Act had been acknowledged by Federalists to impose restrictions on freedom of speech, but in February 1799 they argued that it actually extended freedom of speech.

Related to the new rationale for the Sedition Act, the Report of 1799 also did away with the contingent arguments that leading Federalists advanced in July 1798, instead basing the reasoning for the Sedition Act on more timeless considerations. The new rationale and its timeless nature meant that a Republican response was all the more necessary.

As is clear from the debates of July 1798, Republicans were actively opposed to the Sedition Act. James Madison and Thomas Jefferson, the leading Republicans, were not in the House of Representatives to argue the case against the Sedition Act, but both took active measures against it. The Kentucky Resolutions, adopted in November 1798, and the Virginia Resolutions, adopted in December 1798, were countermoves against it, inspired by Republicans and Jefferson and Madison, in particular. However, the two resolutions broadened the debate from freedom of speech to the question of States' rights and failed to win extensive support in other States. It is also worth noting that in Congressional elections in the immediate aftermath of the Sedition Act the Federalist party, the party behind the Sedition Act, strengthened its grip on Congress.

In the wake of the cool response of other States to the Kentucky and Virginia Resolutions of 1798, Jefferson suggested a meeting in September 1799 between himself, James Madison and one or two other leading Republicans, to plan a follow-up move:

Jefferson suggested that the legislatures of Virginia and Kentucky each prepare a
resolution answering state criticisms of the Virginia and Kentucky Resolutions of

1798, documents that would include a reiteration of their protest against the unconstitutionality of the Alien and Sedition Acts as well as a statement of their continued attachment to the Union. To this Jefferson later added the wish that the resolutions should also treat the "new pretensions to a common law of the U.S." (Mattern et al. eds., 1991, 304))

The task of writing the Virginia Report fell to James Madison:

JM [James Madison, JR] was too astute a politician not to see that the threat of secession would obscure the constitutional issues being debated and would play into the hands of Federalists, who had already condemned Virginians as disloyal unionists. Furthermore, given Jefferson's official position as vice president and his hesitation in exposing himself to prosecution under the Sedition Act, the task of writing the Virginia resolution was assumed by JM, who was also strategically placed in the assembly to push the resolution through committee and floor battles. (Mattern et al. eds., 1991, 304))

Thus was born the Report of January 7, 1800, more commonly known as the Report of 1800. The purpose of this chapter is to examine such parts of it as are directly relevant to shedding light on Madison's concept of freedom of expression.

The Report of 1800

In the Report of 1800 James Madison addressed the interrelated issues of the Blackstonian concept of freedom of speech and of a presumed Federal common law of libel at length, rejecting these doctrines. Here is Madison's unequivocal repudiation of Blackstone:

The freedom of the press under the common law is, in the defences of the Sedition Act, made to consist in an exemption from all *previous* restraint on printed publications by persons authorized to inspect and prohibit them. It appears to the committee that this idea of the freedom of the press can never be admitted to be the American idea of it; since a law inflicting penalties on printed publications would have a similar effect with a law authorizing a previous restraint on them. It would seem a mockery to say that no laws should be passed preventing publications from being made, but that laws might be passed for punishing them in case they should be made. (Hunt ed. (1906, 386), emphasis in the original)

To establish the distinctive character of the American Constitution, Madison started by discussing the British Constitution:

In the British Government the danger of encroachments on the rights of the people is understood to be confined to the executive magistrate. The representatives of the people in the Legislature are not only exempt themselves from distrust, but are considered as sufficient guardians of the rights of their constituents against the danger from the Executive. Hence it is a principle, that the Parliament is unlimited in its power; or, in their own language, is omnipotent. Hence, too, all the ramparts for protecting the rights of the people—such as their Magna Charta, their Bill of Rights, &c.—are not reared against the Parliament, but against the royal prerogative. They are merely legislative precautions against executive usurpations. Under such a government as this, an exemption of the press from previous restraint, by licensers appointed by the King, is all the freedom that can be secured to it. (Hunt ed. (1906, 386))

Here is how the American Constitution and American practices differ from those of Great Britain:

In the United States the case is altogether different. The People, not the Government, possess the absolute sovereignty. The Legislature, no less than the Executive, is under limitations of power. Encroachments are regarded as possible from the one as well as from the other. Hence, in the United States the great and essential rights of the people are secured against legislative as well as against executive ambition. They are secured, not by laws paramount to prerogative, but by constitutions paramount to laws. This security of the freedom of the press requires that it should be exempt not only from previous restraint by the Executive, as in Great Britain, but from legislative restraint also; and this exemption, to be effectual, must be an exemption not only from the previous inspection of licensers, but from the subsequent penalty of laws. (Hunt ed. (1906, 386 f.))

Madison then concludes:

The state of the press, therefore, under the common law, cannot, in this point of view, be the standard of its freedom in the United States. (Hunt ed. (1906, 387))

Madison develops the argument further:

It may be alleged that although the security for the freedom of the press be different in Great Britain and in this country, being a legal security only in the former, and a constitutional security in the latter; and although there may be a further difference, in an extension of the freedom of the press, here, beyond an exemption from previous restraint, to an exemption from subsequent penalties also; yet that the actual legal freedom of the press, under the common law, must determine the degree of freedom which is meant by the terms, and which is constitutionally secured against both previous and subsequent restraints. (Hunt ed. (1906, 387))

Madison then proceeded to give a substantive reason why it is necessary to have a broader view of freedom of expression in the United States than in Great Britain:

The nature of governments elective, limited, and responsible in all their branches, may well be supposed to require a greater freedom of animadversion than might be tolerated by the genius of such a government as that of Great Britain. In the latter it is a maxim that the King, an hereditary, not a responsible magistrate, can do no wrong, and that the Legislature, which in two-thirds of its composition is also hereditary, not responsible, can do what it pleases. In the United States the executive magistrates are not held to be infallible, nor the Legislatures to be omnipotent; and both being elective, are both responsible. Is it not natural and necessary, under such different circumstances, that a different degree of freedom in the use of the press should be contemplated? (Hunt ed. (1906, 387 f.))

Madison thus established an important principle for open societies and democratic countries: where governments are elective and accountable for their actions, a degree of freedom of expression is needed that is different from countries where the rulers are not responsible for their actions or are only responsible to themselves, as in monarchical Great Britain, and further, that the degree of freedom of expression should be higher in the former than in the latter.

Madison proceeded explicitly to argue that some degree of abuse of freedom of speech is welcome and to point to the beneficial effects of this freedom:

Some degree of abuse is inseparable from the proper use of every thing, and in no instance is this more true than in that of the press. It has accordingly been decided by the practice of the States, that it is better to leave a few of its noxious branches to their luxuriant growth, than, by pruning them away, to injure the vigour of those yielding proper fruits. And can the wisdom of this policy be doubted by any who reflect that to the press alone, chequered as it is with abuses, the world is indebted for all the triumphs which have been gained by reason and humanity over error and oppression; who reflect that to the same beneficent source the United States owe much of the lights which conducted them to the ranks of a free and independent nation, and which have improved their political system into a shape so auspicious to their happiness? Had "Sedition Acts," forbidding ever publication that might bring the constituted agents into contempt or disrepute, or that might excite the hatred of the people against the authors of unjust or pernicious measures, been uniformly enforced against the press, might not the United States have been languishing at this day under the infirmities of a sickly Confederation? Might they not, possibly, be miserable colonies, groaning under a foreign yoke? (Hunt ed. (1906, 389))

Madison had a further argument for rejecting the narrow view of the freedom of the press, as embodied in the Sedition Act. Madison wrote:

... it is manifestly impossible to punish the intent to bring those who administer the Government into disrepute or contempt, without striking at the right of freely discussing public characters and measures; because those who engage in such discussions must expect and intend to excite these unfavorable sentiments, so far as they may be thought to be deserved. To prohibit, therefore, the intent to excite those unfavorable sentiments against those who administer the Government, is equivalent to a prohibition of the actual excitement of them; and to prohibit the actual excitement of them is equivalent to a prohibition of discussions having that tendency and effect; which, again, is equivalent to a protection of those who administer the Government, if they should at any time deserve the contempt or hatred of the people, against being exposed to it by free animadversions on their characters and conduct. Nor can there be a doubt, if those in public trust be shielded by penal laws from such strictures of the press as may expose them to contempt, or disrepute or hatred, where they may deserve it, that, in exact proportion as they may deserve to be exposed, will be the certainty and criminality of the intent to expose them, and the vigilance of prosecuting and punishing it; nor a doubt that a government thus intrenched in penal statutes against the just and natural effects of a culpable administration will easily evade the responsibility which is essential to a faithful discharge of its duty. (Hunt ed. (1906, 396 f.))

Here Madison provided a cogent argument against the Sedition Act and similar censorship laws designed to ensure that no publication should bring the rulers of the state into disrepute. As Madison argues, to prohibit the intent to excite unfavorable sentiments is to prohibit the excitement of such sentiments, and to prohibit the excitement of such sentiments is to protect those in authority from such sentiments even when they are deserved. Madison's position reminds us of one of the reasons adduced in chapter 1 for why freedom of speech is essential to the proper functioning of democratic and representative self-government, and it demonstrates a down-to-earth sense of realism about those in authority. By contrast, a philosophical position favoring the Sedition Act and similar censorship laws reflects an idealistic and naive view of the nature of rulers.

Chapter 10

The Federalist Attempt to Perpetuate the Sedition Act

In January 1801, when the Presidential election had not yet been resolved, Federalists made a determined effort to perpetuate the Sedition Act. The Act, as enacted into law in the summer of 1798, was approaching the end of its life, for it was set to expire on March 3, 1801, and Federalists were thus running short of time. They still had a small majority in the House of Representatives in January 1801 when they made their move, but they were also aware of the prospect of losing it soon and of the Republican party, after their gains in the elections of 1800, forming the new administration at the Federal level.

In John C. Miller's account there were several factors motivating the behavior of Federalists in seeking to perpetuate the Act. He observes that the Sedition Act had been "their darling" and writes:

> In seeking to perpetuate the Sedition Act, the Federalists were not ... acting out of mere perversity; there was sound reason for their stand on this issue. They were resolved, above all, to make no deathbed repentance; consistency and the stiff upper lip to the end. Moreover, it was clear that if they could but transmit the Sedition Act to the Republicans, they would embarrass and confuse the incoming administration; Jefferson, if he remained true to his principles, would be reluctant to invoke this Act against his political enemies. (Miller (1951, 228))

Miller writes further:

> Nor is it extraordinary that the Federalists, if they were to be punished for libel and sedition, preferred to take their medicine from the Federal government rather than from the states. In falling victims to their own law, they would at least have the satisfaction of confirming the principles for which they had fought. (Miller (1951, 228))

And finally, Miller suggests that Federalists "assumed that if truth were admitted as a defense — as it was under the Sedition Act — few, if any, of them would be convicted of libeling Jefferson. Nothing they could say about him would be as awful as the truth" (Miller (1951, 228)).

To the points made by Miller, a consideration should be added on the basis of the present study. It may be recalled that in July 1798 the Federalist rationale for the Sedition Act was in large measure founded on contingent factors — the threat of war against France, in particular — but that there was a major change in the Federalist rationale soon afterwards. In the Report of February 1799, the reasoning for the Sedition Act was detached from contingent factors and was instead based on timeless principles. Since the rationale for the Sedition Act was now based on timeless principles, it made sense to propose making the Act permanent.

The debates to be examined here took place on during the period from Wednesday, January 21, 1801 to Friday, January 23, 1801. Arguments used in them are examined here.

The Debate of January 21, 1801

On January 21, 1801 the House went into a Committee of the Whole to consider a resolution reported by the Committee of Revised and Unfinished Business "that it would be expedient to renew the law in addition to the act for the punishment of certain crimes against the United States" (*Debates* (1851b, 916)), as the Sedition Act was called. The debate started as follows:

> Mr. PLATT, chairman of the committee, explained the reasons of the committee for proposing a resolution for its continuation. The only arguments that could be adduced against it were, as to the constitutionality and as to the expediency of the measure. That it was Constitutional, he contended could be well and plainly proved without entering into the question upon the grounds and proofs exhibited at the period of the original passage of the bill, from the decision in its favor, after a lengthy examination in both Houses of Congress, and its adoption into a law. Added to this was the solemn decision and concurrence of the Judiciary.
>
> After these deliberate decisions in favor of it, to doubt the constitutionality of this law would be absurd. To those who took every occasion to show their opposition to the Government, and were accustomed to vilify the conduct of its warmest adherents, this law must be obnoxious; but those who considered the Government a blessing, and worthy the protection of a free people, must approve of the provisions of this law, as one of the most valuable institutions in its support. (*Debates* (1851b, 916 f.))

Platt started his speech with a noteworthy shifting of the presumption of proof, for instead of saying what there was in favor of the measure, Platt says that there were "only" two arguments against it.

Platt went on to employ the fallacy of *ad verecundiam*. The appeal was to the authority of both Houses of Congress, which is a high and credible enough authority, to be sure, but the argument was still fallacious because when Congress approved the measure in July 1798, it had a time limit on it, being set to expire on March 3, 1801, and now in January 1801 they were debating the application of the Act with respect to a later time period.

There is also an *ad hominem* attack on the opponents of the bill in this extract. When Platt terms them as people "who took every occasion to show their opposition to the Government," he is engaging in denigrating their character and branding them as unreasonable.

Mr. Platt went on to give a more positive argument for continuing the Sedition Act:

> To those who believed the rule of common law of force and effect in the United States, this law must be truly gratifying. By the common law two practices were established, which this law effectively removed by its ameliorating provisions. First, the common law rejected the evidence of truth in cases of libel. Secondly, the court had unlimited authority to ascertain the penalty. By this law the truth must be given in evidence, and the penalty is ascertained. He trusted that whilst the liberty of speech and of the press (privileges to be prized above all others) were made secure, the House would see the propriety of preventing the unlimited abuse of this blessing, so injurious to the preservation of social order—an abuse which was to be judged as to its extent by an impartial jury—a privilege by which are secured to every individual, and to the Government, equal rights. (*Debates* (1851b, 917))

The original Federalist rationale for the Sedition Act – that it needed to be introduced in order to restrict what might otherwise be published in the press – is found towards the end of the extract quoted. However, the passage also echoes the shift in public Federalist arguments for the Sedition Act. Platt now publicly spells out the Federalist presumption that there was a common law of libel in operation at the Federal level.

Proceeding from that presumption, Platt argued that the Sedition Act in fact alleviated the common law of libel, that is, that without the Sedition Act the crimes covered in the Sedition Act would be dealt with more stringently than with the Sedition Act. The plausibility of the argument is undercut by the controversial and dubious nature of the presumption and by the ineffectiveness of the putatively ameliorating provisions of the Sedition Act, as discussed in chapter 8.

Representative Davis spoke next, opposing the continuation of the Sedition Act. He characterized the difference between Federalists and Republicans as follows:

> If that gentleman [Representative Platt, J.R.] and his friends intend to act honestly, why do they wish this law to hide their actions? Why lay the hands of power on the lips of the people, who ought to have the right of examining their political

conduct and approving or condemning it? While they boast of honesty, why skulk in darkness and shelter behind a sedition law? In my opinion, this neither argues honesty, nor is ominous of good; at all events this is the true difference between the parties in this House. That gentleman and his friends form a party who wish to conceal their public conduct from the prying eyes of the public, and who say, if you see you shall not speak. Myself and my political associates are willing to spread our actions before the tribunal of the people, and to be judged by them. Now let the world judge who are the honest men, we, who expose our actions to public view, and say to them, judge, and approve or condemn us for our deeds; or those who say, be silent; we are above you; if you open your lips the penalty of the law shall be inflicted on you. (*Debates* (1851b, 918))

It is clear from Davis's remarks here that his perception of the Federalist objective with the continuation of the Sedition Act was to restrict the flow of information, not to alleviate the effects of a presumed Federal common law of libels. This perception of Davis's part is natural because Republicans in general did not believe in a Federal common law of libels.

He also made this point, in response to Representative Platt:

The gentleman from New York says, that those who consider Government an evil will vote against this law. I consider good Government a blessing, and am, therefore, willing to let the people examine freely and fairly the fruits of Government. Those who wish to make it a curse, wish also to conduct it out of the sight of those immediately interested in its operations. This hidden way of conducting the concerns of the nation will never be pleasing to the free people of America. (*Debates* (1851b, 919))

Davis thus rebutted the Federalist charge that those opposed to the law were opposed to all government, by making a plea for openness in government.

Representative Randolph, speaking against the motion, said in part:

He would not enter into a view of the unconstitutionality of the law. How strongly soever the gentleman supposed that question to have been decided by the Congress who passed the law, he would tell that gentleman and all his adherents, that he had a still higher tribunal to appeal to—one higher than they could produce: he meant the American people. Their voice was more powerful than that of those courts and this President, to whom the gentleman referred. (*Debates* (1851b, 919 f.)).

Randolph's argument suggests that there was a measure of popular dissatisfaction with the continued operation of the Sedition Act.

Roger Griswold, a Federalist, spoke next. Like Platt, he proceeded from the presumption that if the Sedition Act were not continued, there would be a Federal common law of libels that would be harsher than the Sedition Act:

> It was a well known fact that at common law the truth could not be given in evidence; it was equally well known, that the punishment for crimes was left undefined, ... To continue the right of giving truth in evidence, and to keep the power of prescribing a punishment with the Legislature, he hoped the law would be re-enacted. (*Debates* (1851b, 921))

Representative Nicholson, speaking next, argued against continuing the Sedition Act. He said in part:

> The first fact he noticed was, the arraignment, trial, and conviction of a member of the House, who was committed under the care of a severe keeper, to an unwholesome and loathsome dungeon, and the treatment of that member whilst in confinement; in all of which were evinced a spirit of party highly unworthy the character this country ought to bear. (*Debates* (1851b, 922))

Nicholson referred to the prosecution of Matthew Lyon, a sitting member of the House of Representatives, who had been jailed for expressing opinions that were mildly critical of the Adams Administration. Nicholson appealed against the partisan spirit of that trial.

Nicholson went on to rebut one of the putatively alleviating provisions of the Sedition Act:

> It was and might be further argued, that the act was only aimed at false and malicious libels, tending to defame the Government. He granted it; but who were to be the judges? The bench themselves; they perhaps might be the subjects of animadversion, but if not, were the creation of the person grieved. By then the materiality of the testimony, which ought to go to the jury, was to be judged, and, therefore, the principle that the truth might be given in evidence, was of but little importance, if that truth was not suffered to appear. (*Debates* (1851b, 922))

Samuel Dana, a prominent Federalist, spoke next, in support of continuing the Sedition Act. In his view judges, nominated by the President, were "men of the most profound wisdom and integrity" (*Debates* (1851b, 924)).

Benjamin Huger, speaking next, opposed continuing the Sedition Act. He viewed it as restricting freedom of speech and argued that the times had changed:

> For his part, he had heard nothing, nor could he see any reason, which led him to think such a measure either expedient or necessary at the present moment. Granting that Congress possessed the Constitutional power of laying some restrictions on the licentiousness of the press, and of punishing libels, yet it certainly does not follow of

course, that they must necessarily, at all times and on all occasions, carry that power into operation. (*Debates* (1851b, 926))

He went on to argue against "an appearance of restraint":

As little noise has been made with respect to this law in the State he had the honor of representing, as in perhaps any part of the Union; yet it certainly had occasioned some uneasiness in the public mind even there; and he was convinced the great majority of his constituents would not willingly see it again renewed at the present time. He would venture even to go so far as to say, that the freedom of speech and of the press, though carried even to a certain degree of licentiousness, was in general deemed preferable by them to anything like an appearance of restraint on either. (*Debates* (1851b, 927))

He further remarked that "it was ... well known, that those who were about to enter into the administration of the Government had on all occasions declared themselves openly and unequivocally hostile to the principles of this act" (*Debates* (1851b, 928)).

Representatives Claiborne and Nicholas, the next two speakers, opposed continuing the Sedition Act. The former said in part:

Mr. C. remarked that the conduct of public men should always be investigated; that free investigation was inseparable from a representative Government, and essential to its preservation; that in such investigation base men might resort to calumny, but this was an evil which could not be remedied without rendering insecure a valuable privilege. (*Debates* (1851b, 929))

John Rutledge, speaking next, supported continuing the Sedition Act in force. He discussed a number of individual cases tried under the Sedition Act. He went on to observe:

The truth is, sir, that in those sections of our country where clamors have been raised against this law, everything is disliked and everything is abused which emanates from the Federal Government. (*Debates* (1851b, 932))

Rutledge's remark here is in the light of a broad-brush *ad hominem* fallacy, making wholesale allegations and generalizations about entire sections of the country.

Robert Harper, who had been one of the chief sponsors of the Sedition Act in 1798, spoke next. He devoted much of his speech to discussing and defending trials that had taken place under the Sedition Act. He went on to make a more general point:

The constitutionality of the law has been, on many former occasions, triumphantly established by arguments to which not even the semblance of an answer has been given. Indeed, sir, I have never so lowly appreciated the understandings of those who have clamored about the unconstitutionality of this act, as to suppose that they themselves believed in their objections. I have ever considered those objections merely as instruments for working on the public mind, as party expedients for exciting discontent against those in power and paving the way for their dismissal. I have ever considered the constitutionality of the Sedition act as a mere stalking-horse, behind which to fight the Administration. I believe that it has always been so considered by those who have used it; by those who have most gladly grasped, and most industriously wielded, a weapon whereby they hoped to demolish the power of their political adversaries, and open the way for their own. Hence, sir, and hence alone, the odious epithets which have been heaped upon it, and the tales fabricated about oppressions exercised in the course of its execution. Hence the charge that Congress had no power to make a provision, which rests on the same principle whereon are founded nearly one third of the laws in our code; and which cannot be distinguished, and has never been attempted to be distinguished, from the first section of the same act—the section against seditious meetings—about the constitutionality of which a doubt has never been raised. (*Debates* (1851b, 938 f.))

Harper had probably never heard of fallacy theory or informal logic, but his remarks here confirm the salience of the theory of fallacies to the debates on the Sedition Act. Harper was in effect accusing his Republican opponents of having used arguments that were fallacies, in the sense of fallacy theory, as understood in Rudanko (2001), (2003), and in this book. He was saying that his Republican opponents had had a secret agenda all along, that of bringing the Federalist administration into disrepute, and that the arguments against the Sedition Act, whether they concerned questions of constitutionality or other grounds, were "a mere stalking-horse, behind which to fight the Administration" (*Debates* (1851b, 939)). That is, he was alleging that all Republican arguments against the Sedition Act had been fallacious, designed to accomplish their secret goal of wresting power from the Federalist party.

To make an allegation of such magnitude and of such generality about the pervasiveness of fallacies in Republican arguments may be taken to betray a sense of frustration about the failure of Federalist policies. Or the analyst may wonder if such a suggestion about opposition techniques may be self-reflexive and reveal a guilty feeling about his own techniques to get the Sedition Act approved and extended.

Like other Federalists, Harper took it for granted that there was a Federal common law of libels and at the end of his speech, he joined in the sentiments expressed earlier in the debate by Platt that the Sedition Act protected freedom of speech:

> ... I shall now, while I may, vote for the continuance of that law, which mitigates the
> rigor of the common law in this respect, and protects the liberty of the press and of
> opinion, by enacting that the truth may be given in evidence on indictment for libels
> against the Government. (*Debates* (1851b, 940))

Harper's speech concluded the proceedings of the House of Representatives on
Wednesday, January 21, 1801.

The Debate of January 22, 1801

The debate was resumed on Thursday, January 22, 1801. The first speaker was
James Bayard, a well-known Federalist, who had been active in earlier debates and
in attempting to expel Matthew Lyon from the House of Representatives (see
Rudanko (2001, chapter 5). He referred to that case in the course of his remarks:

> He then took a view of the case, in which, it was said, an honorable gentleman
> of that House had been fined in a large sum, and confined in a loathsome dungeon.
> What, he inquired, was the object in mentioning that case? A libel was published
> against the Government; a jury of the country declared it to be false, scandalous, and
> malicious, and yet the punishment is complained of as a hardship! As well might we
> be told of hardship when a felon suffers for his crime; or that it was hardship when a
> vote was taken for expelling the honorable gentleman from this House.
>   Will you say that the judge and jury were corrupt? The House by a vote
> sanctioned their decision. He was convicted by a fair trial, and if the court did wrong,
> so did this House. (*Debates* (1851b, 947))

Two fallacies may be alleged here. The claim that Lyon "was convicted by a fair
trial," involves begging the question. This has been characterized as follows:

> The fallacy of begging the question, also called petitio principii or arguing in a circle,
> occurs in an argument where a premise depends on the conclusion, or is even
> equivalent to it, in such a way that the requirement of evidential priority is violated.
> Evidential priority requires that the premises be better known or more firmly
> acceptable than the conclusion subject to doubt. [Note omitted, J.R.] (Walton (1995,
> 49))

In his statement Bayard was taking the fairness of the trial for granted, even
though it was a point at issue. That it was a point at issue was indeed recognized by
Bayard, when he appealed to the vote of the House, where a majority of members

supported expelling Lyon from the House because of the earlier conviction under the Sedition Act. The reference to the decision of the House might be seen in the light of the fallacy of *ad verecundiam*. It is open to question whether a vote by the House of Representatives is a proper authority by which to judge the question of whether a criminal trial had been conducted in a fair way, especially bearing in mind that the motion in the House of Representatives had been on the issue of whether to expel Lyon. This is related to the question of the fairness of the trial, but it is not identical to it. (See also Albert Gallatin's response below).

It may also be noted that the way that Bayard's appeal was couched might be viewed as a further fallacy, of the type that Two Wrongs Make One Right: "if the court did wrong, so did this House" (*Debates* (1851b, 948)).

Bayard also addressed the question of why, in his view, the Act was constitutional and necessary:

> It is said, the law is unconstitutional. He thought a sound mind might be intuitively convinced of the contrary. If such a law is necessary to preserve and continue the Constitution, it is Constitutional. It is necessary to defend the Government from the attempts of assassins. If you allow the Government to be brought into contempt, the Constitution will become a baseless fabric, and in time will vanish away. The right to make such a law he thought was clearly and expressly given in the 8th section of the 1st article of the Constitution, which says "Congress shall have power to make all laws which shall be necessary and proper for carrying into execution the foregoing powers, and all other powers vested by this Constitution in the Government of the United States, or in any department or officer thereof." In his opinion, the law is so essentially necessary, that without it the Government would be paralyzed and stripped of all defence. He thought it unnecessary to trouble the House with further argument, as those offered were sufficient in his opinion; he knew of no stronger ones. (*Debates* (1851b, 948))

The reference to the article of the Constitution involves interpretation but it would be unreasonable to view it as a fallacy. However, the fallacy of *ad consequentiam,* or that of elided slippery slope, is salient because of the exaggerated nature of the dire consequences that Bayard was conjuring up when he claimed that without the Sedition Act "the Government would be paralyzed" or that the Constitution "will vanish away."

Bayard went on to say "that if this law is permitted to expire, the common law will be in force, by which fine and imprisonment are unlimited, and truth is not allowed to be given in justification" (*Debates* (1851b, 948)), thus voicing his adherence to the Federalist presumption of a Federal common law of libel, and claiming that the Sedition Act alleviated its force.

Here is how Bayard saw the options before the country:

To paralyze the General Government, and confide all power to the State courts, is a system invariably pursued by some gentlemen on this floor. He was not, therefore, surprised that they should wish it not to be the law of the courts of the United States. We must, however, have one of the two alternatives; take the common law or have no law. The courts must be either despotic, or bound by the common law. (*Debates* (1851b, 950))

Bayard was here engaging in another rhetorical trick, in claiming — reductively — that there were only two alternatives: either accept the common law at the Federal level, with a continued Sedition Act, or there will be no law and despotism will ensue.

Here is the record of the end of his speech:

Mr. B. concluded by saying: If I am correct in my position that the common law is the law of the land, the Sedition law ought to be continued, because it limits and softens the penalties in cases of libels, which are very harsh according to the common law. The gentleman from Virginia has rightly appreciated my motives in wishing to renew this law, when a different administration is to take charge of the public welfare. (*Debates* (1851b, 950))

Albert Gallatin, a Republican, spoke next, partly in response to Bayard. He denied the assertion by Bayard and by other Federalists that a decision not to continue the Sedition Act would mean that there would be a Federal common law of libel in existence, saying that he "did not think the courts of the United States would at once assume jurisdiction over libels, according to the common law, in case this act was not revived" (*Debates* (1851b, 951)).

He went on to take up another point made specifically by Bayard:

The gentleman from Delaware had mentioned the case of a member of this House who had been punished under the Sedition law, and considered the vote given for his expulsion as a sanction of the decision of the judge and jury. In such instances the Constitution declared that two-thirds were necessary for a decision. This was provided on the principle that such might be the prevalence of party spirit, that a majority would agree to expel without well-grounded reasons. The vote was, therefore, a nullity, as two-thirds did not agree to it. (*Debates* (1851b, 951))

Gallatin thus challenged Bayard's argument from appeal to authority head-on. Bayard had appealed to the vote of the House on a motion to expel Lyon as confirming the justice of a court decision and the appropriateness of how the Sedition Act had been operating, thus providing grounds for continuing the Act. However, Gallatin pointed out that the vote on a motion to expel Lyon had in fact failed and had thus been "a nullity." In terms of fallacy theory, Gallatin was saying that the appeal to authority was a fallacy in the present case, since the vote had been a failure. The exchange between the two Congressmen concerning the vote on a motion to expel Lyon illustrates one way in which the nature of the authority appealed to can be contested.

Gallatin went on to develop his more general objection to continuing the Sedition Act:

> Mr. G. considered laws of this kind as the means of introducing party views into courts of justice; and that it was only in such cases that any danger of partiality was to be apprehended; here it is to be apprehended, unless you can suppose judges become different men merely by being placed on the bench. It is also certain that the jury must be composed of one or the other party, and is, therefore, incompetent to decide upon opinions. He did not suppose them intentionally doing wrong. He asked if any gentleman in the House would be willing to be tried for a libel by a jury chosen from the members of it who are of different political opinions? He confessed he would not. (*Debates* (1851b, 951))

At the end of his speech Gallatin argued that the Sedition Act had been executed "only by punishing persons of politics different from those of the administration, and that "if the Sedition law was adopted only as a part of defensive measures, it is no longer necessary" (*Debates* (1851b, 952)).

Harrison Otis, one of the strongest supporters of the Sedition Act and of the philosophical position underlying it, as has become clear in the debates considered here, spoke next. He strongly supported the continuation of the Act in the present debate. He said in part, in justifying the Act and what he took to be its constitutionality to critics:

> But above all it was a sufficient answer on this occasion, that the wisdom of a former Legislature, composed of a majority of the present members, after great deliberation, had adopted this law, as a safeguard against the rapid progress of an unparalleled licentiousness, which threatened the subversion of the Constitution. When it is considered, further, that this House has, in two instances, affirmed the constitutionality of this most salutary law; once by rejecting a resolution to repeal it, and once by sanctioning the judgment of a court in the case of the member from Vermont; was it reasonable to expect that a majority would be formed ready to abandon a doctrine to which they had, with such solemnity, subscribed their assent? For these reasons, said Mr. O., we are acquitted from all obligation to justify the act upon the principles which gave it birth, and in my turn I call on gentlemen to prove the mischiefs and grievances which have sprung from it. Let them show that it has been used as an instrument of oppression, and the scourge of innocence. Let them demonstrate its inexpediency from the practice that has arisen under it, and if they succeed in this attempt, then, indeed, with a good countenance, they may call on us to

rescind it. (*Debates* (1851b, 953))

Otis shifted the burden of proof in the debate here. The members of the House of Representatives were debating a resolution concerning the expiry date of the Sedition Act. This had been set for March 3, 1801. In a reasonable argumentative dialogue, those in favor of having the Sedition Act in force after March 3, 1801 might have been expected to produce reasons for prolonging the Act. However, Otis argued that supporters of the Sedition Act were "acquitted from all obligation to justify the act upon the principles which gave it birth"; instead, he called on those who did not want to make the Sedition Act permanent to justify their position, as if the Act had always been without a time limit and as if the debate were about rescinding the Act and not about its prolongation. The shifting of what may be termed the default assumption may be a fallacy in itself, though it does not seem to feature among the traditional arsenal. It might be called the fallacy of shifting the default position.

Otis was led to his position by another fallacy, or by a combination of two fallacies. His appeals to previous decisions of the House of Representatives, first in establishing the Sedition Act and then in not repealing it, brings to mind the fallacies of arguing from precedent and of *ad verecundiam.* What undermines the appeals is that the House of Representatives established the Sedition Act in circumstances different from those in January 1801 and that those circumstances were cited as a reason for the Act, as was seen in chapter 7. For their part, the decisions not to rescind the Act concerned the Act as it was at the time of the decisions: it is recalled that the Act included the key provision according to which it was set to expire on March 3, 1801. The application of fallacy theory thus exposes flaws in Otis's reasoning.

In the further course of his speech, Otis accused Republicans of engaging in prosecutions for libel in State courts, and brought up the Federalist claim that the Sedition Act might serve as a shield against prosecution, presuming that if the Sedition Act were not continued, there would automatically be a Federal common law of libel in the land.

He concluded his speech by arguing for the continuation of the Sedition Act as follows:

> I see nothing in the Constitution or the law, or in the practice under the law, that should induce those who once supported it, to desert it at this moment. The prospect of a war with France is more remote, but the temper of the times is not changed, nor the licentiousness of the press controlled. We may want this law as a coat of armor to defend us from persecution, and we should be willing to give to the new Administration the means of protection that have been provided for their predecessors. For these reasons my vote will be given in favor of the resolution. (*Debates* (1851b, 958))

Otis thus addressed his plea primarily to the loyalty of his fellow Federalists, saying that those who had supported the Sedition Act should continue to do so.

The Debate of January 23, 1801

The debate on the continuation of the Sedition Act was resumed the following day, Friday, January 23, 1801. The first speaker was Henry Lee. He spoke in favor of the Sedition Act, saying in part that "he would not hesitate for a moment to say that this law ought to be made perpetual" (*Debates* (1851b, 960)). One of the points made by him in the course of his speech was the argument from precedent from the State level. Speaking about what he took to be the duty to protect the Government, he said in part:

> He was surprised at his colleague's objection and that of the gentleman from Pennsylvania, when it was made so evidently to appear by the gentleman from Maryland (Mr. DENNIS) that such a protection was afforded by their own State constitution and law! This truth was too strong to be resisted. He believed it to be the case in almost every State. And if so in the individual States, why should not so valuable a remedy be afforded to the Government of the Union? This was the charter of our venerable sires, and what principle should withhold this disposition from their enlightened and experienced sons? Why should that be denied to the supreme Government which every member of the House, and which every individual in the Union, enjoyed? Why should gentlemen deny that to the Federal Government which was granted to the separate Governments? (*Debates* (1851b, 961 f.))

The argument may be seen as an instance of the fallacy from analogy, of the type that came up in the discussion of the debate of July 5, 1798.

Representative Macon, a Republican opposed to continuing the Sedition Act, spoke next. He made a point about a shift in Federalist argumentation for the Sedition Act that has also emerged in the present study:

> It was a little curious to observe the manner in which those who approved the law, changed the ground on which they defended it at different times. It originated in the days of alarm, and was then supported as a part of a system of defence against France; at that time this common law of the United States, of which we now hear so much, was not talked of. The second time it was before the House, it was brought up by many petitions from the people in different States, praying for its repeal; then, too, it was considered as a part of the system of defence, and, as the dispute with France was not settled, it was said to be improper to repeal it. At the last session, when a motion was made to repeal the second section of the act, the law was then supported

on this reason, to prevent the operation of the common law, and to afford the gentlemen themselves the liberty of expressing their sentiments, if founded in truth, and expressed with decency; and so it is that the friends of order and good government now want the Sedition law to protect themselves. (*Debates* (1851b, 963))

Macon also took up one of the arguments put forward by Otis, which was mentioned above:

We have been told by a gentleman that he heretofore voted for this law, and that therefore he should vote for it again. Surely there cannot be a worse reason for a vote than this; it goes on the principle of never changing, and if a law be once passed, it must remain a law forever. *(Debates* (1851b, 965))

Macon did not speak in terms of fallacies, but the conjunction of the fallacies from precedent and *ad verecundiam* yields the state of affairs the he describes: if a law is passed, "it must remain a law forever."

Representative Dennis spoke next, in support of extending the life of the Sedition Act. He voiced worries about what he took to be a consequence of a new and more generous interpretation of the liberty of the press:

Sir, there is no crime which will not be sanctioned by this new doctrine of the liberty of the press: Treason itself may be committed with impunity, if such principles be established. According to the construction which by some is affixed to the amendment to the Constitution, Congress can make no law in any manner affecting the press, because they say every such law must amount to an abridgment thereof. (*Debates* (1851b, 967))

There is an air of fallacious exaggeration about the dire consequences envisaged by Dennis as flowing from what he took to be a new interpretation of the liberty of the press: "Treason itself may be committed with impunity" (*Debates* (1851b, 967)).

In the further course of his remarks Dennis referred to the State of Virginia:

By the 12th article of the Declaration of Rights of Virginia, it is provided: "That the liberty of the press is one of the great bulwarks of liberty, and can never be restrained but by despotic Governments." It is believed that this expression does not substantially vary from the amendment of the Constitution, which says, among other things, "that Congress shall make no law abridging the freedom of speech or of the press." (*Debates* (1851b, 968))

He went on to note that Virginia also had a law of libel and a law against spreading false news and said: "There is no man who will contend, that if the

Sedition act be a violation of the amendment of the Constitution, these several acts of the Virginia Assembly are not equally infractions of their Bill of Rights" (*Debates* (1851b, 970)).

Dennis's argument brings to mind the fallacy of "Two Wrongs Make One Right." The analogy that he drew, similar to what Otis said on July 10, 1798 (see chapter 7), is also suspect, given that only the First Amendment places a well-defined restriction on the power of the Legislature. For his part, Dennis hastened to add that neither Virginia nor the Federal government had exceeded their powers.

Dennis went on to quote from a letter by Thomas Jefferson dated August 28, 1789, in which Jefferson made the following comment on what would become the first Amendment:

> "I like it as far as it goes, but I should be for going further; for instance, the following alterations and additions would have pleased me: Article 4. 'The people shall not be deprived of the right to speak, to write, or otherwise publish anything but false facts, affecting injuriously the life, liberty, property, or reputation of others, or affecting the peace of the Confederacy with foreign nations." (*Debates* (1851b, 971))

The quotation does represent Jefferson's sentiments, and it does appear that his view of freedom of speech was more narrow that Madison's. However, the appeal to Thomas Jefferson's authority as part of an argument for prolonging the life of the Sedition Act is dubious because of Jefferson's active and visible opposition to the Sedition Act during the time when the Act had been in force. There may have been a degree of desperation creeping into the Federalist ranks at this point.

The last speaker in the debate on Friday 23, 1801 was Matthew Lyon. It is almost poetic justice that the member of the House of Representatives who had been imprisoned under the Sedition Act should speak last in a debate intended by its Federalist originators to perpetuate the duration of the Act. He gave the House of Representatives an account of his ordeal, including the charges against him and the nature of the trial against him (see Rudanko (2001, chapter 5)). He also gave a graphic depiction of his time in a jail cell, "the common receptacle of thieves, murderers ..." (*Debates* (1851b, 975)). He concluded as follows:

> Unless gentlemen can defend these things let them speak no more of the superiority of this law over the common law, nor vindicate it upon the limits of its punishment being assigned, the contrary of which I think my experience abundantly proved. (*Debates* (1851b, 975))

Out of context, an argument containing details of unpleasant personal experiences might be thought of as an instance of the fallacy of *ad misericordiam*, or appeal to pity: "we should have sympathy for the wretched situation of this person *P*, therefore we ought to accept the conclusion of the argument that *P* maintains" (Walton 1998a, 22)). However, in the present case the account is pertinent to the issue at hand, the nature of the Sedition Act and the way it had been administered against an opposition member of Congress, and it can hardly be considered a fallacy here.

After Lyon's speech the House, as a Committee of the Whole, voted on the resolution for continuing the Sedition Act. It passed, by the casting vote of the Chair. The House then voted on the same resolution. The result was 48 yeas and 48 nays, and the resolution passed again, by the casting vote of the Chair.

Summing Up

The attempt to perpetuate the life of the Sedition Act beyond the expiry date of March 3, 1801 is not a very well-known event in United States history. Yet it was a serious attempt, with some of the most prominent Federalists in the House of Representatives taking part, including Representatives Harper, Otis and Bayard. And in January 1801 Federalists wishing to make the Sedition Act permanent were still able to prevail in the vote, concluding the debate. It was only after the election of Thomas Jefferson on February 17, 1801 that the majority of the House of Representatives finally turned against the Sedition Act on February 21, 1801 (Rudanko (2003, 128 f.)).

In the debates of January 1801 the most typical Federalist argument for continuing the Sedition Act was two-pronged: on the one hand they argued that the Act was needed to curb what they considered the licentiousness of the press, and on the other, they argued that without a Sedition Act, there would be in operation a Federal common law of libel, with even harsher penalties. The latter argument, though conspicuously absent from the debates in July 1798, was prominent in Federalist rhetoric by February 1799. Perhaps its increased prominence might have had to do with Federalist fears that the incoming Republican administration might adopt the Federalist idea of a Federal common law of libels and prosecute their opponents.

There were also a fair number of rhetorical tricks or fallacies in Federalist arguments in January 1801. One of these was Otis's attempt to shift the burden of proof to those who did not want to continue the Act, as if the Act had not been set to expire on March 3, 1801. Otis declared flat out that since the law had been passed and upheld in the past, it should be continued now.

Federalists were also in the habit of engaging in expressions of fear and foreboding about the prospect of the expiry of the Sedition in such exaggerated terms that they brought to mind the fallacy of *ad consequentiam* or of elided slippery slope. Thus Bayard opined that if the Sedition Act were not made permanent, despotic rule would follow.

For their part, Republicans strenuously denied any intention that they would adopt the idea of a common law of libel at the Federal level. They stressed their commitment to the idea that there was no Federal common law of libel and that there was no need for the Sedition Act either. They also lamented the partisan way in which the Sedition Act had been applied, against Republicans only. They also made the point that the Sedition Act had been passed "in the days of alarm," but that the alarm had subsided.

Representative Macon also noted how Federalist arguments for the Act had shifted: when the Sedition Act was introduced, the presumed Federal common law of libel "was not talked of," as Macon put it, but the idea that there was such a law had become a prominent claim later, with the consequence that the Sedition Act was now portrayed by Federalists as protecting freedom of speech. The shift in Federalist argumentation that Macon identified is also highlighted by the present study. As was seen in chapter 7, in the debates of July 1798 Federalists shied away from asserting that there existed a Federal common law of libel. However, as seen in chapter 8, only some seven months later the presumption of such a Federal law of libel formed a foundation of the Federalist rationale for the Sedition Act.

Chapter 11
Concluding Observations

Introduction

Two broad themes of this book are examined in this concluding chapter. The first of these is that of the question of original intent and the second that of the constitutive power of the Bill of Rights. (On the theme of fallacies in selected Congressional debates of the period, see Rudanko (2003).)

The Question of Original Intent

The question of original intent needs to be approached with some caution. Describing the intention of a human being who proposes a certain measure or a course of action is a complex matter, and in the present case, the question is complicated by the passage of time, for we are dealing here with intentions over two centuries ago. We are also dealing here with the intentions of a body of men, but at the same time, the intentions of James Madison assume a critical importance, in view of his critical role in the enactment of the Bill of Rights.

What can be said with certainty is that Madison's Report of 1800 does afford a fully explicit insight into his thinking at that time. There is no doubt that he advocated a very liberal view of freedom of speech and of the press at that time. As noted in chapter 9, he explicitly rejected the Blackstonian view that freedom of the press meant the absence of inspection prior to publication:

> This security of the freedom of the press requires that it should be exempt not only from previous restraint by the Executive, as in Great Britain, but from legislative restraint also; and this exemption, to be effectual, must be an exemption not only from the previous inspection of licensers, but from the subsequent penalty of laws. (Hunt ed. (1906, 387))

Madison also provided a fully worked out justification for this view of freedom of the press, relating it to the nature of American representative government, where both the executive and legislative branches of the government are elective and accountable:

> In the United States the executive magistrates are not held to be infallible, nor the
> Legislatures to be omnipotent; and both being elective, are both responsible. Is it not
> natural and necessary, under such different circumstances [different from the
> circumstances in Great Britain, JR], that a different degree of freedom in the use of
> the press should be contemplated? (Hunt ed. (1906, 388))

Madison's puts his point in the form of a rhetorical question, but the question
amounts to the assertion 'surely it is natural and necessary that such a higher degree
of freedom should exist in the United States.

Madison is also quite explicit that freedom of the press, as understood and
advocated by him, involves abuse, and he is ready to countenance it as a matter of
deliberate policy:

> Some degree of abuse is inseparable from the proper use of every thing, and in no
> instance is this more true than in that of the press. It has accordingly been decided by
> the practice of the States, that it is better to leave a few of its noxious branches to their
> luxuriant growth, than, by pruning them away, to injure the vigour of those yielding
> the proper fruits. (Hunt ed. (1906, 389))

The present study also showed how Madison was by no means the only person
in the Republican party to hold a generous view of the freedom of the press at the
time of the Sedition Act. As noted, Representative Livingston, in the debate of July
10, 1798, advocated the position that there was no such thing as a slander against
the Government. And in general a broad view of freedom of the press and of
speech was the Republican position in the debates in the context of the Sedition
Act.

The present study also affords a window into the views held by Madison and
other Republicans several years earlier, in November 1794. It was observed that
several Republican speakers articulated a broad view of freedom of the press and
of speech even at that time. Thus Nicholas observed that "I cannot agree to
persecution for the sake of opinions" (*Debates* (1849, 905)) and Madison weighed
in with "Opinions are not the objects of legislation" (*Debates* (1849, 934)). The
deeper necessity of permitting freedom of speech as a prerequisite for the proper
functioning of representative government may not have been fully worked out —
or may not have been explicitly expressed — by Madison at this time. Yet there is
no mistaking his generous interpretation of the concept of freedom of expression
even in 1794.

Going back by another five years, to the context of the debates for the Bill of
Rights in the summer of 1789, means having to rely on more circumstantial
evidence, when trying to decide on Madison's original intent with this First

Amendment. One way of putting the question is: could he have meant that the First Amendment should endorse the Blackstonian or British view of freedom of speech and of the press, where the concept only meant the absence of prior censorship?

In view of the present study, the answer is that the suggestion that Madison wished to endorse the Blackstonian view with his amendments is an unlikely and unwarranted interpretation of his project. As shown in chapter 3, Madison set up a deliberate contrast between Great Britain and the United States in his major speech on June 8, 1789. He argued that "the freedom of the press and rights of conscience, those choicest privileges of the people, are unguarded in the British Constitution" (Gales (1834, 436)). The clear intent of his amendments was to ensure that those "privileges of the people" should be safeguarded in a more adequate way in the United States than they are safeguarded in Great Britain. It was also emphasized by him that they should be protected against the power of the government, by setting such limits on what the government can do as will be more adequate, once a Bill of Rights is passed, in the United States than in Great Britain, lacking a similar Bill of Rights. To construe his intent as a desire to reproduce the British practice in the United States would be a fanciful interpretation, when he was so anxious to differentiate what he proposed for the United States from British practices.

The interpretation of Madison's intent in 1789 advanced here, with its emphasis on a distinctively American view of freedom of the press, is also supported by a statement that Madison made in his Report of 1800 when looking back on practices in the United States, prior to the Sedition Act:

In every State, probably, in the Union, the press has exerted a freedom in canvassing the merits and measures of public men of every description which has not been confined to the strict limits of the common law. On this footing the freedom of the press has stood; on this footing it yet stands. (Hunt ed. (1906, 388))

Madison's point is supported by a consideration of Federal prosecutions for seditious libel before and after the Sedition Act. It is well known that there was vigorous critical discussion in the press, including criticism of the government in the period between 1791 and 1797. However, there were very few attempts to invoke a presumed Federal law of seditious libel during this time, and the attempts that were made collapsed (cf. Miller (1951, 66, note 29)). After the enactment of the Sedition Act, Federal prosecutions for offences linked to freedom of speech multiplied, even extending to the prosecution of one sitting member of the House of Representatives. Madison was thus stating the truth when, looking back, he noted that "the press has exerted a freedom in canvassing the merits and measures of public men ... which has not been confined to the strict limits of the common law" (Hunt ed. (1906, 388)).

The conclusion here, regarding Madison's views, is that the weight of the evidence favors the view that this framer of the Constitution had a broad view of freedom of speech when proposing his amendments.

As for the view of Federalists, it is clear in the light of this study that in 1799 the Federalist position was that there was a common law of seditious libel in operation at the Federal level in the United States and that the concept of freedom of speech only meant the absence of censorship prior to publication. As a consequence of the doctrine of a Federal common law of seditious libel, Federalists made the claim in 1799 that the Sedition Act "is so far from having extended the law and power of the court, that it has enlarged instead of abridging the liberty of the press" (*Debates* (1851a, 2989)).

In July 1798 Federalists did not assume the doctrine of a pre-existing Federal common law of seditious libel when they enacted the Sedition Act. As detailed in chapter 7, Federalists pushed through the Act with great speed, in spite of the constantly repeated Republican argument that the Act was unconstitutional because of the First Amendment. The present investigation showed how in the debate of July 5, 1798 Federalists were seemingly quite unable to answer the Republican argument. It was observed how at one point in the debate John Allen said bluntly that with the Sedition Act Federalists wanted to "wrest" the press from Republicans.

Given the public nature of debates in the House of Representatives, it is reasonable to suppose that there was pressure on Federalists during and after the debate of July 5, 1798 to find something less discreditable and something more presentable and plausible than John Allen's brutal statement as an answer to the Republican argument that the Sedition Act was unconstitutional. In the debate of July 10, 1798 Federalists did have more sophisticated responses, but the claim is made here that these tended to be fallacious. For instance, it is recalled how Robert Harper was reduced to attempting to draw an analogy between a verbal and a physical assault. For his part, Harrison Otis argued, more subtly, that some States had Constitutions with provisions to protect freedom of the press and to guard against libel and that since it was understood at the State level "that to punish licentiousness and sedition is not a restraint or abridgment of the freedom of speech or of the press" (*Debates* (1851a, 2147)), the same principle should be appropriate at the Federal level. As noted, Otis's analogy is undermined by the pointed and specific nature of the First Amendment.

As far as the purpose of the Sedition Act was concerned, it is possible to say, in the light of the debates of July 5 and July 10, 1798, that there was no ambiguity about the objective of its Federalist sponsors in July 1798. The aim was to impose restrictions on what could be published in the press with impunity, in order to combat what Federalists viewed as the licentiousness of the press. There is no doubt that there was vigorous critical discussion in the press in the 1790s prior to the enactment of the Sedition Act, and the Federalist aim was to place limits on the content of political discussion and on criticism of the Administration. There was to be no censorship prior to publication. Instead, the Sedition Act involved criminal penalties after publication when the content of the opinions expressed was judged to have violated the Act.

The present investigation also revealed how the Sedition Act grew out of earlier Federalist thinking and how the Federalist position on freedom of speech had been more restrictive than the Republican position prior to the context of the debates of the Sedition Act. As shown in chapter 6, Fisher Ames argued in the context of the debates on whether or not to censure Democratic societies in 1794 that what was needed was "genuine" liberty of the press. His meaning was that restraints were needed in relation to what was being practiced by the press at that time.

Federalist reservations about the degree of freedom of speech obtaining in the country in 1794 were clear enough in the debates of November 1794. Going back to the original debates of the summer of 1789, it should be recalled that at that time, Madison was a leading Federalist. Pronouncing on Madison's intentions in 1789 involves a degree of inference; pronouncing on the intentions of other Federalists at that time is an even more difficult enterprise. The present author would speculate that many Federalists probably had a view of freedom of speech that was more restrictive than Madison's view even in 1789.[1] The point never came up in the debates of the summer of 1789. If the speculation is correct, it was fortunate for the project of the Bill of Rights that it never did come up, for even a small diminution of the grudging Federalist tolerance for Madison's project, especially during the long-drawn-out procedural wrangling, might well have terminated the whole project of amendments in the summer of 1789.

The Constitutive Role of the First Amendment

This study also sheds light on the question of why the Sedition Act failed and did not become permanent. How was it that the American Sedition Act proved to be of such short duration, while similar Acts in other countries have proved to be much more enduring? It should be recalled that repressive laws aimed at restricting freedom of speech were enacted both in Great Britain and in the United States in the 1790s, with the Federalist sponsors of the Sedition Act indeed tending to take their cue from similar British laws, which were enacted around 1795.

A first answer to this question may be given as something like "because the Republican Party won Congressional seats in the elections of 1800 and because Thomas Jefferson was elected President in February 1801." There is truth in this answer, but there is still more to be said. Regarding the efforts to suppress freedom of speech in both Great Britain around 1795 and in the United States in 1798, what is intriguing is not so much the concerted nature of these efforts in both countries on both sides of the Atlantic at that times, but rather the contrast in the degree of serious opposition to the repressive measures. In the United States the Sedition Act was approved only by a very small majority in the House of Representatives, and there were repeated calls and petitions for repealing the Act or at least major sections of it. By contrast, in Great Britain opposition to similar measures to restrict public criticism of the Government was insignificant or marginal in character.

No doubt the fact that Great Britain was actually at war with France was a factor (cf. Elkins and McKitrick (1993, 712 f.)). However, at a deeper level the strength of the popular and Congressional opposition to the Sedition Act in the United States was probably also due to a freer climate of public discussion fostered by the simple and yet compelling language of the First Amendment. By contrast, Great Britain lacked a comparable Bill of Rights — and continues to lack it to this day, as does every other country in the world — which meant that proponents of freedom of speech in that country did not have the kind of constitutional provision that Republicans in the United States were able to appeal to and to rally around in their fight for freedom of speech.

The present investigation certainly showed the power of the First Amendment in Congressional debates. As shown in chapter 7, it was the constant theme of Republicans in the debates of July 1798 and it continued to form the basis of the Republican claim that the Sedition Act was unconstitutional. It was also an argument that Federalists trying to justify the Sedition Act had constantly to struggle with. In the debate of July 5 they tried to ignore it, but Republican appeals to it were so persistent that it was impossible to ignore. If there had been no Bill of Rights as part of the Constitution at the time of the Sedition Act, it is entirely possible that the American Sedition Act might have proved to have as much longevity as similar Acts in other countries. Even if the Sedition Act had been repealed later, a less open and a more restrictive conception of freedom of speech might well have prevailed in the United States.

It was the existence of the First Amendment that brought the question of what freedom of speech meant into a sharper focus in the debates on the Sedition Act. It also made the question of what abridging freedom of speech means into a well-defined issue. The constitutive power of the First Amendment deserves to be recognized, further highlighting the stature of James Madison as the father of the Bill of Rights and as the father of freedom of speech.

Notes to Chapter 11

1. Even Thomas Jefferson, while a strong proponent of a Bill of Rights in the run-up to 1789 and a strong opponent of the Sedition Act, had a view of freedom of speech that appears to have been more narrow than that of his friend Madison. Here is Jefferson writing to his friend on August 28, 1789, suggesting language that would have modified the text of what was to become the First Amendment:

'The people shall not be deprived or abridged of their right to speak to write or *otherwise* to publish any thing but false facts affecting injuriously the life, liberty, property, or reputation of others or affecting the peace of the confederacy with foreign nations. (Hobson et al. (1979, 363, the word "otherwise" underlined by Jefferson))

Madison deserves to be commended on his judgment not to adopt the language of his friend when formulating and working on his amendment to guarantee freedom of speech.

Bibliography

Allan, Keith. 1986. *Linguistic Meaning.* Volume 2. London: Routledge.

Bentham, Jeremy. [1824, 1952] 1962. *The Handbook of Political Fallacies.* Revised and edited by Harold A. Larrabee. New York: Harper Torchbooks.

Blackstone, William, Esq. [1769] 1966. *Commentaries on the Laws of England.* Book the Fourth. London: Dawsons of Pall Mall. A reprint of the first edition with supplements [Oxford: Clarendon Press].

Bowling, Kenneth. 1990. *Politics in the First Congress, 1789-1791.* New York: Garland Publishing.

Brown, Penelope and Stephen Levinson.1987. *Politeness. Some Universals in Language Use.* Cambridge: Cambridge University Press.

Cooke, Jacob E., ed. 1961. *The Federalist.* Middletown, Conn.: Wesleyan University Press.

Copi, Irving and Keith Burgess-Jackson. 1996. *Informal Logic.* Third edition. Upper Saddle River, New Jersey: Prentice Hall.

Dascal. Marcelo and Alan G. Gross. 1999. "The Marriage of Pragmatics and Rhetoric," *Philosophy and Rhetoric,* volume 32, 107-130.

Dauer, Manning. 1953. *The Adams Federalists.* Baltimore: The Johns Hopkins Press.

Debates. 1849. *Debates and Proceedings in the Congress of the United States; with an Appendix, containing Important State Papers and Public Documents, and all the Laws of a Public Nature, with a Copious Index. Third Congress: Comprising the Period from December 2, 1793, to March 3, 1795, inclusive.* Compiled from Authentic Materials. Washington: Printed and Published by Gales and Seaton.

Debates. 1851a. *The Debates and Proceedings in the Congress of the United States; with an Appedix, containing Important State Papers and Public Documents, and all the Laws of a Public Nature; with a Copious Index. Fifth Congress, comprising the period from May 15, 1797, to March 3, 1799, inclusive.* Compiled from Authentic Materials. Washington: Printed and published by Gales and Seaton.

Debates. 1851b. *The Debates and Proceedings in the Congress of the United States; with an Appendix, containing Important State Papers and Public Documents, and all the Laws of a Public Nature, with a Copious Index. Sixth Congress, Comprising the Period from December 2, 1799, to March 3, 1801, inclusive.* Compiled from Authentic Materials. Washington: Printed and published by Gales and Seaton.

DenBoer, Gordon, editor, Lucy Brown, associate editor, Charles Hagermann, editorial assistant. 1984. *The Documentary History of the First Federal Elections 1788-1790.* Volume II. Madison, Wisconsin: The University of Wisconsin Press.

Elkins, Stanley and Eric McKitrick. 1993. *The Age of Federalism.* New York: Oxford University Press.

Gales, Joseph. 1834. *The Debates and Proceedings in the Congress of the United States; With an Appendix, Containing Important State Papers and Public Documents and All the Laws of a Public Nature; with a Copious Index.* Volume 1, *Comprising (with volume II) the Period from March 3, 1789, to March 3, 1791, Inclusive.* Compiled from authentic materials, by Joseph Gales, Senior. Washington: Gales and Seaton.

Godin, Benoit. 1999. "Argument from Consequences and the Urge to Polarize," *Argumentation,* vol. 13, 347-365.

Hobson, Charles, William Rachal, Robert Rutland, and Jeanne Sisson, eds. 1979. *The Papers of James Madison,* Volume 12, *2 March 1789-20 January 1790 with a Supplement 24 October 1775-24 January 1789.* Charlottesville: University Press of Virginia.

Hunt, Gaillard. 1906. *The Writings of James Madison. Comprising his Public Papers and his Private Correspondence, including Numerous Letters and Documents Now for the First Time Printed.* New York: G. P. Putnam's Sons.

Ilie, Cornelia. 1994. *What Else Can I Tell You? A Pragmatic Study of English Rhetorical Questions as Discursive and Argumentative Acts.* Stockholm: Almqvist & Wiksell International.

Letters = Letters and Other Writings of James Madison, Fourth President of the United States. In Four Volumes. Published by Order of Congress. Vol. 1, 1769-1793. 1865. Philadelphia: J. B. Lippincott & Co.

Levin, Bernard. 1991. "Even about the Dead They Lie," *The Times* (August 1, 1991), 14.

Lloyd, Gordon and Margie Loyd. 1998. *The Essential Bill of Rights. Original Arguments and Fundamental Documents.* Lanham: University Press of America.

Mattern, David B. et al. eds. 1991. *The Papers of James Madison, Volume 17.* Charlottesville and London: University Press of Virginia.

Miller, John C. 1951. *Crisis in Freedom.* The Alien and Sedition Acts. Boston: Little, Brown and Company.

Miller, John C. 1997. "Alien and Sedition Acts," entry in *The Encyclopedia Americana, International Edition.* Complete in Thirty Volumes. Danbury, Connecticut: Grolier Incorporated.

Miller, William Lee. 1992. *The Business of May Next. James Madison and the Founding.* Charlottesville: University Press of Virginia.

Nowak, John and Ronald Rotunda. 1991. *Constitutional Law.* Fourth Edition. St.

Paul: West Publishing Co.

Pope, Emily. 1976. *Questions and Answers in English.* The Hague: Mouton.

Quirk, Randolph, Sidney Greenbaum, Geoffrey Leech and Ian Svartvik. 1985. *A Comprehensive Grammar of the English Language.* London: Longman.

Rudanko, Juhani. 1993. "On Some Aspects of Rhetorical Questions in English," *Studia Neophilologica,* 65, 29-36.

Rudanko, Juhani. 1995. "The Bill of Rights in the Balance: the Debate of June 8, 1789," *Multilingua,* volume 14, 391-409.

Rudanko, Juhani. 1997 *Linguistic Analysis and Text Interpretation: Essays on the Bill of Rights and on Keats, Shakespeare and Dreiser.* Lanham, Maryland: University Press of America.

Rudanko, Juhani. 2001. *Case Studies in Linguistic Pragmatics: Essays on Speech Acts in Shakespeare, on the Bill of Rights and Matthew Lyon, and on Collocations and Null Objects.* Lanham, Maryland: University Press of America.

Rudanko, Juhani. 2003. *The Forging of Freedom of Speech. Essays on Argumentation in Congressional Debates on the Bill of Rights and on the Sedition Act.* Lanham, MD: University Press of America.

Rutland, Robert. 1983. *The Birth of the Bill of Rights, 1776-1791.* Boston: Northeastern University Press.

Searle, John. 1969. *Speech Acts. An Essay in the Philosophy of Language.* Cambridge: Cambridge University Press.

Smith, James Morton. 1956 *Freedom's Fetters. The Alien and Sedition Laws and American Civil Liberties.* Ithaca, New York: Cornell University Press.

Smith, Jeffery. 1988. *Printers and Press Freedom.* New York: Oxford University Press.

Smolla, Rodney A. 1992. *Free Speech in an Open Society.* New York: Alfred A. Knopf.

Stephenson, Carl and Frederick Marcham, eds. 1972. *Sources of English Constitutional History.* Volume 1. *A Selection of Documents from A.D. 600 to the Interregnum.* Rev. Ed. New York: Harper and Row.

Trenchard, John and Thomas Gordon, eds. 1971 *Cato's Letters. Essays on Liberty, Civil and Religious, and Other Important Subjects.* Four Volumes in Two. New York: Da Capo Press.

Walton, Douglas. 1995. *A Pragmatic Theory of Fallacy.* Tuscaloosa: The University of Alabama Press.

Walton, Douglas. 1996a. *Argumentation Schemes for Presumptive Reasoning.* Mahwah, New Jersey: Lawrence Erlbaum Associates.

Walton, Douglas. 1996b. "Practical Reasoning and the Structure of Fear Appeal Arguments," *Philosophy and Rhetoric,* vol. 29, 301-313.

Walton, Douglas. 1998a. *The New Dialectic: Conversational Contexts of Argument.* Toronto: University of Toronto Press.

Walton, Douglas. 1998b. *Ad Hominem Arguments.* Tuscaloosa: The University of
   Alabama Press.
Whately, Richard. [1827] 1975. *Elements of Logic.* A Facsimile Reproduction of
   the 2nd Edition published in 1827 by J. Mawman, London. Delmar, New York:
   Scholars' Facsimiles & Reprints.

Author Biographical Sketch

The author, born in 1948, received his degree of Doctor of Philosophy from the University of Tampere, Finland, in 1977. He was Associate Professor of English at the same university from 1979 till 1998. Since 1998 he has been Professor of English at the same university. His publications include *Complementation and Case Gammar* (Albany, New York: SUNY Press, 1989), *Pragmatic Approaches to Shakespeare* (Lanham, MD: University Press of America, 1993), *Prepositions and Complement Clauses* (Albany, New York: SUNY Press, 1996), and *Case Studies in Linguistic Pragmatics* (Lanham, MD: University Press of America, 2001). He is also the author of numerous articles in scholarly periodicals, including *English Studies, Language and Style,* and *Multilingua.*

Index